Poe and the Printed Word

Edgar Allan Poe continues to be a fascinating literary figure to students and scholars alike. Increasingly the focus of study pushes beyond the fright and amusement of his famous tales and seeks to locate the author within the culture of his time. In *Poe and the Printed Word*, Kevin J. Hayes explores the relationship between various facets of print culture and Poe's life and works by examining how the publishing opportunities of his time influenced his development as a writer. Hayes demonstrates how Poe employed different methods of publication as a showcase for his verse, criticism, and fiction. Beginning with Poe's early exposure to the printed word, and ending with the ambitious magazine and book projects of his final years, this reappraisal of Poe's career provides an engaging account that is part biography, part literary history, and part history of the book.

KEVIN J. HAYES is Associate Professor of English at the University of Central Oklahoma. His most recent books include *A Colonial Woman's Bookshelf* (1996), *Folklore and Book Culture* (1997), and *Melville's Folk Roots* (1999), his third book on Herman Melville. He also edited *Henry James: The Contemporary Reviews* (1996).

List continues at end of book

POE AND THE PRINTED WORD

KEVIN J. HAYES

CAMBRIDGE
UNIVERSITY PRESS

PUBLISHED BY THE PRESS SYNDICATE OF THE UNIVERSITY OF CAMBRIDGE
The Pitt Building, Trumpington Street, Cambridge, United Kingdom

CAMBRIDGE UNIVERSITY PRESS
The Edinburgh Building, Cambridge, CB2 2RU, UK   http://www.cup.cam.ac.uk
40 West 20th Street, New York, NY 10011–4211, USA   http://www.cup.org
10 Stamford Road, Oakleigh, Melbourne 3166, Australia

First published 2000

Printed in the United Kingdom at the University Press, Cambridge

Typeset in Baskerville 11/12.5pt   [CE]

A catalogue record for this book is available from the British Library

Library of Congress cataloguing in publication data
Hayes, Kevin J.
Poe and the printed word / Kevin J. Hayes.
p.   cm. – (Cambridge studies in American literature and culture)
Includes bibliographical references and index.
ISBN 0 521 66276 1
1. Poe, Edgar Allan, 1809–1849 – Authorship.
2. Poe, Edgar Allan, 1809–1849 – Books and reading.
3. Publishers and publishing – Maryland – Baltimore – History – 19th century.
4. Poe, Edgar Allan, 1809–1849 – Knowledge – Book industries and trade.
5. Authors and publishers – United States – History – 19th century.
6. Literature publishing – United States – History – 19th century.
7. Fantasy literature, American – History and criticism.
8. Authors, American – 19th century – Biography.
I. Title.   II. Series.
PS2636.H39   2000
818'.309 – dc21   99–16684   CIP

ISBN 0 521 66276 1 hardback

In honor of
Lawrence C. Wroth

Contents

Preface

Modern criticism often ignores the significance of the printed page. Such neglect is partially understandable. As literary texts grow in reputation, they are perpetuated in numerous popular and scholarly editions. Texts become increasingly removed from the form of their original publication, and these removals affect interpretation. The appearance of the printed page, however, shapes the reader's understanding of the text it contains. "The Balloon Hoax" provides a useful example. In most modern editions of Edgar Allan Poe's short stories, its text is uniform with the rest of the pieces in the collection. Each story appears in the same-sized type with identically spaced margins and the same or similar headings. The uniform appearance of the work among other short stories removes any doubt about its fictional nature. So does its title. Originally, it was not called "The Balloon Hoax." It only gained that title in the oral culture *after* its fictional status became known. Containing the word "hoax," the title lets readers know the story is undoubtedly a product of Poe's imagination.

The story's first appearance in print was designed to make it closely resemble a factual account. Poe convinced Moses Y. Beach, editor of the New York *Sun*, to publish it as part of an *Extra Sun*. In terms of format, the story looked similar to any of the day's newspaper articles. It had a dateline as well as a multi-part headline characteristic of urgent news with bold-faced capitals, bold italics, and exclamation marks. The story was set in multiple columns, and the paper included other items, as any paper would. It also contained a woodcut illustration of the model balloon on which the full-scale one purportedly was based. The woodcut image made the technology Poe described more tangible and added further credence. When it first appeared, the hoax was a success, and many people accepted it as truth until they heard reports to the contrary. Unlike his earlier balloon story, "Hans Phaall," this new article contained nothing beyond the pale of contemporary scientific technology. Well aware that an ocean-crossing balloon was feasible, Poe had only to convince his readers. The story's publication as a newspaper extra, however, even more than its realistic detail, made it convincing. Had the work appeared in another medium, say as a magazine article or a separately published pamphlet, few contemporary readers would have been duped. The newspaper extra was the medium for urgent news. Perhaps more than its text, the story's printed appearance made the hoax successful.

Sensitive to the impact of print on interpretation, Poe developed as a writer, in part, by allowing changes in print culture to shape his work. In the present study, I examine the interrelationship between various facets of print culture and Poe's writings – verse, criticism, and fiction. Organized thematically, this volume devotes different chapters to separate print genres or to separate aspects of Poe's life and works. It is also organized in a rough chronological order, starting with Poe's early exposure to the printed word and ending with the ambitious magazine and book projects of his final lustrum. In a way, the present study can be considered a focused biography, for it examines Poe's life and work as they specifically relate to contemporary print culture. Part biography, part literary history, and part history of the book, this volume examines Poe's art and thought from a new perspective.

While I assume my readers are generally familiar with Poe's work, it is not essential to have read all of his writings to follow this book. I have tried to give enough background information to allow initiates to read with ease, yet not so much to weary seasoned Poe scholars. The volume has been designed for a wide readership: undergraduates taking their first survey course in American literature, graduate students, Poe scholars, historians of the book, or anyone who appreciates Poe's writings and enjoys learning more about the man and his *oeuvre*. Though this book specifically concentrates on Poe's relationship to contemporary print culture, it also serves as a general overview of his writing.

The first chapter, "The Student and the Book," examines Poe's earliest contacts with the printed word, looking at the books he read as a student in England and Virginia. Poe's British education opened his eyes to the world of books, and he read a variety of schooltexts and rudimentary literature there. Returning to Richmond, Virginia, he continued his schooling and gave serious attention to the ancient classics. At the same time he taught himself the major contemporary poets and essayists. Poe's Richmond education prepared him well for the University of Virginia where he took classes in ancient and modern languages and continued to read widely outside the classroom. Poe's early reading experiences convinced him of the value of the printed word, not only to disseminate ideas but also to bring alive the world of the imagination, a world where the only entrance requirement is literacy. An earlier version of the first part of this chapter appeared as "Poe's Earliest Reading" in *English Language Notes*, and I am grateful to the editors for granting permission to reprint the article here in a significantly revised and expanded form. The second half of this chapter was originally presented as "Poe's College Reading" at the American Renaissance Conference at Cancun, Mexico, in December 1997. The remainder of the present work appears before the public for the first time.

Poe began writing verse at an early age. According to one story, he had written enough poems as a Richmond schoolboy to consider publishing them in collected form. His teacher dissuaded him from making such private effusions public at the time, but before he was out of his teens Poe's first collection of poetry would appear in print. Once he began publishing his verse, however, Poe did not publish every poem he wrote, for he shrewdly recognized that while some kinds of verse should be made public, others should remain in manuscript. Chapter 2, "Poetry in Manuscript and Print," looks at how Poe's verse reflected the interrelationship between manuscript and print culture. In so doing, it draws upon the work of Donald H. Reiman and his distinction between private, confidential, and public documents. While Poe's poetry reveals his awareness of the differences between manuscript and print culture, in his prose he sometimes challenged the boundaries between the two in such works as "Autography" and "Marginalia."

Poe lived in Baltimore after he left the army and before he entered West Point, and he returned there after being dismissed from the military academy. As Lawrence C. Wroth explained many years ago, Poe's Baltimore was a lively and cultured place. Early on, the scant evidence indicates, Poe mixed with the cultured crowd, but after his return from West Point his scraggly and bepatched condition sometimes made him embarrassed to be seen in polite society. Nevertheless, as chapter 3, "Baltimore Book Culture," suggests, Poe took every chance he could to continue reading old books and to keep up with the latest publications. He developed friendships with local booksellers and members of the Baltimore literati which gave him knowledge he could put to good use later. Though little is known about Poe's day-to-day life in Baltimore, the wide-ranging knowledge of books he revealed when he began writing for the *Southern Literary Messenger* shortly before and after he left Baltimore, suggests that his reading there had been extensive.

John Pendleton Kennedy, Poe's most important literary contact in Baltimore, helped him secure the editorial position with the *Messenger*. Poe's tenure with the magazine was the single most important experience shaping his attitude toward contemporary print culture. I do not devote a separate chapter to the *Southern Literary Messenger*, but, in a way, every following chapter reflects Poe's experience there. Chapter 4, "Booksellers' Banquet," begins with a brief summary of Poe's experience at the *Messenger*, but, for the most part, it treats one night in Poe's life, the night he attended a lavish dinner sponsored by New York's publishers and booksellers. Many of the city's and the country's most important authors and editors came. Poe had read much of their work and corresponded with several of them as part of his editorial duties at the *Messenger*, yet he had met few, if any, of the day's notable literati. Those Poe had treated harshly in his critical notices would scarcely have welcomed him to the table, but others respected his hard-nosed style and had said so in print. All in all, the occasion reflected the exuberant feelings of literary nationalism prevalent throughout the country. The contagious exuberance gave Poe hope for literary success.

Poe had the opportunity to meet the Harper brothers at the Booksellers' Dinner, and that same year they accepted his book-length *The Narrative of Arthur Gordon Pym* for publication. Chapter 5, "The Novel," expands on Bruce I. Weiner's work treating *Pym* as well as Weiner's study of Poe as a literary professional. The chapter title is a *double entendre*, for it refers to *Pym*, the one book-length narrative Poe completed, yet it also looks at Poe's attitude toward the novel as a literary genre. Much work has been done on the composition of *Pym* as well as Poe's use of sources. Here, I pay closer attention to Poe's inspiration for the book, the experiences he had and the books he read which motivated him to a task unprecedented in his personal experience, the writing of a novel. I also examine how contemporary readers received *Pym*, specifically looking at how their attitudes toward the novel-as-genre shaped their understanding of Poe's book. The chapter closes with a discussion of the second and only other book-length work of fiction Poe attempted, the *Journal of Julius Rodman*, and looks at some reasons why Poe ultimately eschewed the novel for the short story.

Chapter 6, "Poe's Library," is, perhaps, a misnomer, for poverty prevented Poe from ever assembling a fine collection of books. Yet Poe did keep some books on hand he needed in his work, and when he was active in an editorial capacity, he received many review copies from the day's leading publishers. True, these did not stay in his possession for long before they went the way of the secondhand shops. Much of the chapter is devoted to Poe's thoughts about books as part of the material culture. "The Philosophy of Furniture" contains Poe's fullest statement on the subject, yet he supplied a handful of other comments concerning the effect the appearance of a shelf of books could have on a reader. The chapter closes with a brief discussion of how Poe used the image of the private library in his fiction.

One extremely influential development in book production occurred at a crucial point in Poe's development as a writer: the pamphlet novel. This new format marked the beginning of the cheap paperback of modern times. Countless foreign authors appeared in pamphlet novels and thus undermined the literary efforts of many American authors. As chapter 7, "Cheap Books and Expensive Magazines," shows, Poe's decision against novel writing and his efforts to own and edit an expensive, high-quality magazine were, in part, a reaction against the pamphlet novel.

Chapter 8, "The Road to *Literary America*," looks at Poe's attitudes toward writing literary history and traces his long-term desire to write a book-length work describing American literature. The project underwent many changes as Poe conceived and reconceived it. He partially realized it in his periodical series, "The Literati of New York City," but he never completed the book. The periodical series created much controversy. Though I do not treat the details of the controversy here – a century and a half later it all seems a little sordid – I do discuss the reasons why the series so upset its subjects. My conclusion provides some general thoughts on Poe's attitude toward the book in general and, in so doing, attempts to sort out the ambivalence Poe felt toward the book during his professional career.

Thanks go out in several directions. First, I would like to thank the compilers of the *National Union Catalog*. I would also like to thank the folks at OCLC for establishing Worldcat. These two bibliographic works have greatly facilitated the present study. I emphasize my gratitude here, for, though I have relied on these two sources, I have found it impracticable to cite them separately for each piece of information I have used from them. This note of thanks, therefore, must serve in lieu of further documentation. I also thank the Huntington Library for granting me permission to reprint excerpts from a manuscript in their possession. Furthermore, I thank Ellen R. Cordes at the Beinecke Library, Yale University for her assistance. I also thank Benjamin Franklin Fisher for reading the manuscript and providing many useful suggestions. At Cambridge University Press, I am grateful to Terence Moore, Leigh Mueller, Ray Ryan, Robyn Wainner, and Michelle Williams. Finally, I thank my parents for their help and encouragement along the way.

Oklahoma City   Kevin J. Hayes

Abbreviations

BAL	Blanck, Jacob, and Michael Winship. *Bibliography of American Literature.* 9 vols. New Haven: Yale University Press, 1955–1991.
Brevities	Poe, Edgar Allan. *The Brevities: Pinakidia, Marginalia, Fifty Suggestions, and Other Works.* Ed. Burton R. Pollin. New York: Gordian Press, 1985.
Collected Works (Mabbott)	Poe, Edgar Allan. *Collected Works of Edgar Allan Poe.* Ed. Thomas Ollive Mabbott. 3 vols. Cambridge: Belknap Press of Harvard University Press, 1969–1978.
Complete Works (Harrison)	Poe, Edgar Allan. *Complete Works of Edgar Allan Poe.* Ed. James A. Harrison. 17 vols. 1902. Reprinted, New York: AMS, 1965.
Essays and Reviews	Poe, Edgar Allan. *Edgar Allan Poe: Essays and Reviews.* Ed. G. R. Thompson. New York: Library of America, 1984.
Letters	*The Letters of Edgar Allan Poe.* Ed. John Ward Ostrom. 1948. Reprinted, with supplement. 2 vols. New York: Gordian Press, 1966.
Log	Thomas, Dwight and David K. Jackson. *The Poe Log: A Documentary Life of Edgar Allan Poe 1809–1849.* Boston: G. K. Hall, 1987.
SLM	*Southern Literary Messenger*

CHAPTER I

The student and the book

I loitered away my boyhood in books, and dissipated my youth
in reverie . . .

"Berenice"

Ellis and Allan, a Richmond, Virginia, import/export firm established by Charles Ellis and John Allan in 1800, became profitable
enough during the following decade and a half for the partners to
decide to open a London office after the War of 1812 had ended. In
1815, John Allan left Richmond for London, taking with him his
family: his wife Frances; her unmarried sister, Ann "Nancy" Valentine, who had long been a member of their household; and Edgar
Poe, the young boy John and Frances had unofficially adopted some
years before. After spending time in Scotland, they reached London
in the first week in October. By month's end, they had found
lodgings in Bloomsbury. Allan wrote home to his business partner,
describing his family and their cozy accommodations, depicting
himself seated "by a snug fire in a nice little sitting parlour in No. 47
Southampton Row, Russel[l] Square where I have procured Lodgings for the present with Frances and Nancy Sewing and Edgar
reading a little Story Book."[1]

That young Poe was busy reading is unstartling. John Allan had
already recognized the child's precocity and purchased some books
for him before they left the United States.[2] The books Allan had
purchased, schooltexts by the English grammarian Lindley Murray,
may have been useful for Poe's education, yet they would hardly
have appealed to him as much as the day's storybooks. Allan
obviously acquired additional volumes for the boy during their first
months in Great Britain. The storybook young Poe was reading in
late October could have been any one of several recently published
chapbooks. He later expressed his familiarity with *Sinbad the Sailor*

and *Jack and the Beanstalk*; new London editions of these two works appeared the year the Allan family came to England.[3] So did new editions of *The History of Little King Pippin* and *Tom Thumb*. (In one of his lectures, Poe would praise a "penny edition of Tom Thumb."[4]) *Mother Goose's Melody*, a work Poe would mention in "The Literary Life of Thingum Bob," appeared in a London edition the following year.[5]

Thomas Love Peacock's *Sir Hornbook, or, Child Launcelot's Expeditions: A Grammatico-Allegorical Ballad*, which went through two editions in 1815, combined grammar and adventure to create a work with greater appeal for a six-year-old than Murray's *Grammar*. As the poem begins, Childe Launcelot approaches the castle of Sir Hornbook who joins the young knight and leads him on a series of adventures, encountering such valiant knights and ladies fair as Sir Syntax and his love, Lady Prosody, and culminating at the Muses' gates where Sir Hornbook leaves the youthful knight:

> Childe Launcelot pressed the sacred ground,
> With hope's exulting glow;
> Some future song perchance may sound
> The wondrous things which there he found,
> If you the same would know.[6]

James Pedder's *The Yellow Shoe-Strings, or, The Good Effects of Obedience to Parents* had appeared in 1814 and had quickly become a popular book among English children or, more precisely, a popular book for British parents to give to their children. Reviewing one of Pedder's subsequent works, Poe wrote that the author was "well known in England, as the composer of one of the most popular juvenile books of the day, 'The Yellow Shoe-strings' – three words familiar in nursery annals. To indite a really good work of this kind is a task often attempted in vain by men of high literary eminence. In truth the qualifications for success depend not a little upon a clear head, but still more upon a warm heart."[7] The work's didactic sentimentalism has doomed it to obscurity since, yet Poe remembered *The Yellow Shoe-Strings* with fondness. His kind words, however, may have been personally motivated. During the 1830s, Pedder moved his family from England to Philadelphia, and Poe developed a close friendship with him and his daughters, Anna and Bessie, who occasionally aided the impoverished Poe family and to whom he inscribed a copy of *Tales of the Grotesque and Arabesque* in 1839.[8]

Some literary classics of the previous century were available in highly abridged versions designed for young readers and illustrated with woodcuts. In 1815, chapbook editions of Daniel Defoe's *Moll Flanders* and *Robinson Crusoe* were published in London, as they had been for many years. Poe later read an unabridged *Robinson Crusoe*, but his first exposure to the work likely came through one of the many chapbook versions. Though John Allan was not much of a literary man, his family would have kept a copy of *Robinson Crusoe*. About the book, Poe later remarked, "It has become a household thing in nearly every family in Christendom."[9] Writing in the editorial first person plural, Poe recalled his childhood memories of the book with great affection: "How fondly do we recur, in memory, to those enchanted days of our boyhood when we first learned to grow serious over Robinson Crusoe! – when we first found the spirit of wild adventure enkindling within us, as, by the dim fire light, we labored out, line by line, the marvellous import of those pages, and hung breathless and trembling with eagerness over their absorbing – over their enchanting interest!"[10] *Robinson Crusoe* fostered Poe's interest in imaginary voyages, an interest other contemporary publications would have perpetuated. The following year, *The Surprising Adventures of Baron Munchausen*, a highly abridged version of Munchausen's *Travels*, appeared as part of the "New Juvenile Library."

During the spring of 1816, Poe entered the London boarding school of the Misses Dubourg. If he had yet to devote much time to Lindley Murray's textbooks, the school would have given him the opportunity. Murray's *English Spelling-Book; With Reading Lessons Adapted to the Capacities of Children* supplemented his education, but it was not the main spelling book the Misses Dubourg used, for John Allan had to purchase a copy of William Fordyce Mavor's *The English Spelling Book, Accompanied by a Progressive Series of Easy and Familiar Lessons* after Edgar had entered the school. Murray's *The English Reader: Or, Pieces in Prose and Poetry, Selected from the Best Writers*, a work that had gone through numerous editions since its original publication in 1799, introduced Poe to many British belletristic writers. The work was broken down into two parts, prose and verse, and each part was subdivided into separate chapters devoted to different types of writing – narrative, didactic, argumentative, descriptive. The prose section of the book contained quotations from Joseph Addison, Hugh Blair, Oliver Goldsmith, David Hume, and Samuel Johnson, among many others. The poetry section provided generous excerpts from the work of Mark Akenside, William Cowper, John Milton, Alexander Pope, James Thomson, and Edward Young.

While there is no way to know precisely how much attention Poe gave these textbooks during his early years in England, his later writings reveal his familiarity with Murray's works, which would become a kind of touchstone in Poe's criticism. *The English Grammar,* Murray's most well-known schooltext, figures prominently in his review of Theodore S. Fay's *Norman Leslie.* In the review, Poe quibbled with Fay's and, indirectly, with Nathaniel P. Willis's grammar: "As regards Mr. Fay's *style,* it is unworthy of a school-boy. The 'Editor of the New York Mirror' has either never seen an edition of Murray's Grammar, or he has been a-Willising so long as to have forgotten his vernacular language." Poe pointed out several grammatical errors and concluded: "There is not a single page of Norman Leslie in which even a schoolboy would fail to detect at least two or three gross errors in Grammar, and some two or three most egregious sins against common-sense."[11] Another amusing reference to Murray came in a footnote to a poem of Murray's reprinted in the *Southern Literary Messenger.* Poe called Murray "that celebrated grammarian" but ended his footnote with the comment, "It is somewhat remarkable that the present lines involve an odd *grammatical* error of construction in the concluding stanza."[12]

The ease and confidence with which Poe noticed grammatical errors in others' works suggests that he paid close attention to his early schoolbooks. Reviewing Hugh A. Pue's *Grammar of the English Language, in a Series of Letters, Addressed to Every American Youth,* Poe found numerous grammatical errors and concluded that "whether Mr. P.'s queer little book shall or shall not meet the views of 'Every American Youth,' will depend pretty much upon another question of high moment – whether 'Every American Youth' be or be not as great a nincompoop as Mr. Pue."[13] While a good grammarian, Poe nevertheless bristled at the kind of regimentation grammatical rules imposed. In his "Fifty Suggestions," written near the end of his life, he wrote, "Let the noblest poet add to his other excellences – if he dares – that of faultless versification and scrupulous attention to grammar. He is damned at once. His rivals have it in their power to discourse of 'A. the true poet, *and* B. the versifier and disciple of Lindley Murray.' "[14]

Young Poe was introduced to the fundamentals of the Anglican Church at the Dubourg school, too. A *Book of Common Prayer* and a copy of John Lewis's *The Church Catechism Explained by Way of Question and Answer*, a work which had been in use for over a century, were among other expenses John Allan paid to the Dubourgs at the time.[15] Beyond its religious value, the *Book of Common Prayer* would have impressed Poe with the elegance of the English language. Most of the selections in Murray's *English Reader* came from the Augustan Age, but the prose of the Anglican prayer book, with its formal diction and long periods, hearkened back to the Elizabethan.

Poe also studied history and geography with the Dubourgs. He learned geography reading Nicolas Lenglet Dufresnoy's *Geography for Children: Or A Short and Easy Method of Teaching and Learning Geography*, a text in use since the 1730s, and he studied history with Christopher Irving's *A Catechism of the History of England*. Back in the United States, schoolchildren Poe's age were reading native history and geography texts written from highly nationalistic points of view. Unlike so many other Americans who grew up during and just after the War of 1812, Poe expressed little political animosity toward Great Britain. Far from it. His critical writings sometimes encouraged rapprochement between the two countries. Reviewing John Armstrong's *Notices of the War of 1812*, he wrote, "We are grieved . . . to see, even in the opening passages of the work, a piquancy and freedom of expression, in regard to the unhappy sources of animosity between America and the parent land, which can neither to-day nor hereafter answer any possible good end, and may prove an individual grain in a future mountain of mischief."[16] The dearth of American themes and characters in Poe's writings, aspects that have helped his works rise above the jingoistic breast-beating of his contemporaries, can be attributed partially to the cosmopolitan education he received from the Misses Dubourg.

Sometime in late 1817 or early 1818, Poe left the Dubourg school and began attending the Manor House School, Stoke Newington, about four miles from London. The school and its overseer, the Reverend John Bransby, would receive fictional treatment in Poe's "William Wilson." Most of the schoolbooks were the common property of the Manor House School and passed from one student to the next – if Poe's description in "William Wilson" can be believed: "Interspersed about the room, crossing and recrossing in endless irregularity, were innumerable benches and desks, black, ancient, and time-worn, piled desperately with much-bethumbed books."[17] Here, if not before, Poe began learning Latin. On 22 June, 1818,

John Allan wrote to a correspondent, "Edgar is a fine Boy and reads Latin pretty sharply."[18] A good Latin education begins with *Aesop's Fables*, and a copy of *Aesopi Fabulae* formerly in Poe's possession survived into the twentieth century.[19] The Reverend Bransby also exposed his students to British *belles lettres* and Latin verse. Another pupil remembered him as a "thorough scholar" who was "very apt at quotation, especially from Shakespeare and Horace."[20] Poe also continued his study of English history with John Bigland's *Letters on English History, for the Use of Schools* and may have read Bigland's other textbooks treating geography, European history, and natural history.[21]

John Allan was proud of his young foster son's scholarly prowess and often wrote to his uncle William Galt from London to tell him so. In three letters written during a four-month period which included Poe's eleventh birthday, Allan wrote that Edgar "enjoys a good reputation and is both able and willing to receive instruction"; "is a verry fine Boy and a good Scholar"; and "by his own exertions he has repaired many Gaps [in his education] both in general literature and the Sciences."[22] The books young Poe read at Stoke Newington would prepare him for the fine classical education he would receive upon his return to Virginia.

The London office of Allan and Ellis (John Allan had transposed the names in England) proved unsuccessful, so the Allan family returned to Richmond in the summer of 1820. Later that year, Poe began studying with Joseph H. Clarke, a schoolmaster who had recently relocated from Baltimore. In the advertisements for his Richmond school, Clarke stated that he taught the classical languages, writing, arithmetic, bookkeeping, geometry, trigonometry, navigation, surveying, gunnery, optics, astronomy, conic sections, algebra, mechanics, and geography, among many other subjects. Though the list seems hyperbolic, other evidence verifies that he provided his students with a broad education. Clarke, who lived into his tenth decade, recalled Poe reading "Ovid, Caesar, Virgil, Cicero, and Horace in Latin, and Xenophon and Homer in Greek."[23] Though supplying several names, this recollection actually reveals little, for the works of these authors formed the core of any good classical education. John Allan's account books show that he paid Clarke for a copy of *De officiis*, Cicero's ethical treatise written as advice to a son, and an expensive edition of Horace's works.[24] Besides *De officiis*,

Poe read several of Cicero's orations, knowledge of which was required for admission to the day's universities.[25] Ciceronian rhetoric, Marshall McLuhan has argued, significantly influenced Poe's outlook as well as his discursive style.[26]

Clarke also remembered Poe writing verse at the time, so the boy's interest in Horace is understandable. Schoolmate John T. L. Preston recalled Poe's enthusiasm: "He was very fond of the Odes of Horace, and repeated them so often in my hearing that I learned by sound the words of many, before I understood their meaning."[27] When his schoolbooks did not occupy his time, Poe read the important British belletristic writers. Lord Byron was an early favorite, and he admitted having modelled his youthful verse on Byron's. At this time he likely read such other modern British poets as Samuel T. Coleridge, Thomas Moore, and Percy Bysshe Shelley and such essayists as William Hazlitt, Leigh Hunt, and Charles Lamb. Poe also recalled reading Washington Irving in his youth.[28] *The Sketch Book of Geoffrey Crayon* had appeared in parts in 1819 and 1820; from then, complete editions were steadily available.

Poe spent three years at the school, but when Clarke left Richmond to return to Baltimore in 1823, his pupils transferred to William Burke's school. Like Clarke, Burke was a good classicist. Since he had already published a pamphlet, *Prosody of the Latin Language* (Richmond, 1816), Latin-versifying would have occupied a prominent place in Burke's teaching. Poe himself later admitted, "I have made prosody, in all languages which I have studied, a particular subject of inquiry."[29] Poe's extensive discussion of prosody, "The Rationale of Verse," may owe a modest debt to Burke. Later, Burke would publish a basic Latin textbook. The work would appear too late for Poe to use, but it provides a good indication of Burke's teaching approach. Since Burke based his textbook on Thomas Ruddiman's *Rudiments of the Latin Tongue*, a work generations of young Latin scholars had been using since the 1750s, Burke presumably taught from Ruddiman when Poe was his student.

There was little that Poe could learn from Burke that he had not already learned from Joseph Clarke, however. The reminiscence of Andrew Johnston, a fellow student at Burke's school, bears this out: "Poe was a much more advanced scholar than any of us; but there was no other class for him – that being the highest – and he had nothing to do, or but little, to keep his headship of the class. I dare say he liked it well, for he was fond of desultory reading, and even then wrote verses."[30] The relationship between Poe and the world of books Johnston described aptly conveys the attitude toward print culture Poe had formed during his childhood and adolescence. On one hand, books provided systems of knowledge, ways of organizing the world into knowable facts; on the other hand, books freed the imagination, allowing the reader to journey backward to antiquity and forward into the imaginary future. Young Poe may not have articulated himself precisely in these terms, but, as he read Byron while his classmates were reading Ruddiman's *Rudiments*, he understood how the printed word could free as well as constrict the mind.

After opening its doors the year before, the University of Virginia began its second session on 1 February, 1826. The young man destined to become the most famous student matriculating that session had yet to reach Charlottesville, however. Poe did not arrive until mid-February at which time he registered for classes, signing up for Professor George Long's Ancient Languages and Professor George Blaetterman's Modern Languages. Most students took three courses, but, according to Poe, John Allan had not provided him with enough money to afford the tuition for a third class, which would have been mathematics. Nor did Poe have enough money to purchase the textbooks he needed. A week after he had arrived, he wrote home "for some more money, and for books." He continued to write home for more books as needed, including a copy of Tacitus' *Historiae*. Other necessary textbooks Poe purchased locally, buying them on credit at usurious rates.[31]

Outside the University, there were a few places students could go to get books. Retail shops selling general goods stocked some basic school texts: Cicero, Homer, Livy. They also stocked recent novels and other contemporary belletristic works. Jones's bookstore was not far from campus. Since Poe could scarcely afford necessary textbooks, it seems unlikely he made many book purchases beyond the essential, but Jones, if his establishment were anything like other contemporary American bookshops, ran an informal circulating library. Here Poe may have found many books published the year he entered the University, several of which he came to know, including James Fenimore Cooper's *Last of the Mohicans*; Benjamin Disraeli's *Vivian Grey*, a work which Poe would spoof in "King Pest";[32] and Timothy Flint's *Recollections of the Last Ten Years Passed in Occasional Residences and Journeyings in the Valley of the Mississippi*.

One of Poe's acquaintances recalled a local harnessmaker named Hermann Tucker who became successful enough at his trade to be able to expand his retail business into "a sort of curio store filled with second-hand articles." During Poe's time, Tucker's stock included books from a library "which had fallen under the auctioneer's hammer in order to satisfy a plantation debt."[33] According to the recollection, Poe became especially fond of a copy of Hogarth's prints from the library. That Hogarth appealed to Poe is unsurprising – George Bernard Shaw would associate the two.[34] Hogarth's depictions of London streetlife, with all its earthy detail, would have jived with the memories of anyone who spent their childhood there. Since Poe later devoted much thought to printed illustrations when he imagined his ideal magazine, his early attention to Hogarth takes on further significance. Like that of any Virginia plantation owner, the collection Tucker acquired would also have included many historical works and a wide variety of *belles lettres* including the *Spectator*, Chesterfield's *Letters*, Charles Johnstone's *Adventure of a Guinea*, and Laurence Sterne's *Tristram Shandy*, to name a few possibilities among the numerous eighteenth-century belletristic works Poe came to know.[35]

Of all his sources for books, Poe's fellow classmates were his likeliest. Since he had no qualms about borrowing money from other students, it seems unlikely Poe would have refrained from borrowing books from them. Few commodities are easier to borrow (or more difficult to return) than books.[36] Among a group of generally intelligent and well-to-do young men, Poe had the opportunity to talk about literature and exchange ideas with others, the kind of experience John Allan had seldom encouraged. Poe joined the Jefferson Literary Society and became its secretary. Members discussed what books they had read, made recommendations for reading, and shared writings of their own composition.

The attitudes expressed by members of the Jefferson Literary Society are not difficult to guess. Among the various literary genres, the most well respected were poetry and history. Though some eighteenth-century fiction writers had achieved considerable respect – Henry Fielding, Samuel Richardson, Tobias Smollett – fiction, by and large, still held a second-class status as a literary genre. Thomas Jefferson made no place for it in his organizational scheme for the University's library.[37] Writing histories or other non-fiction works was much more highly regarded than fiction-writing. Members of an early nineteenth-century literary society could talk seriously about poetry or history-writing but seldom about novels. Sir Walter Scott, of course, was the major exception among contemporary writers of fiction, but his works were better labelled historical romances than novels. The example of Scott suggested that the only way to make fiction-writing respectable was to steep it in history.

Thomas Goode Tucker, a fellow student, remembered Poe voicing his opinions about literature multiple times. On one occasion, Poe read a lengthy story he had written only to have it laughed down by his friends. He became so incensed that he flung the manuscript into the fire.[38] Tucker further recalled that Poe was "fond of quoting poetic authors and reading poetic productions of his own" and also that he and Poe read the histories of David Hume and John Lingard while at the University of Virginia.[39]

The first three volumes of Lingard's *History of England* appeared in 1819, and additional volumes were published during the 1820s. Lingard's was the first serious, scholarly history of England to appear since Hume's *History of England*. Though Hume's work had achieved status as a literary classic by Poe's day, it was by no means unassailable, and Lingard had set out, unostentatiously and inoffensively, to refute Hume historical era by historical era.[40] Discussing Hume and Lingard during the first half of 1826, Poe and Tucker were absolutely *outré*, for the contemporary British quarterlies were also discussing the relative merits of the two historians. Both the *Edinburgh Review* and the *Quarterly Review* attacked Lingard. Robert Southey, who wrote the *Quarterly Review* article, censured Lingard's treatment of the Reformation. Reading and discussing the two historians, Poe and Tucker kept themselves abreast of one of the day's important literary controversies. Though the quarterlies squabbled over religious issues, Poe may have noticed another key difference between the two works. Lingard's was a political history while Hume had made literary history a part of England's general history, the first important historian to do so.

While comparing Hume with Lingard was in vogue, Hume had long been compared to fellow Scottish historian, William Robertson. Such comparisons appeared in both the British and the American periodicals of Poe's day. A contributor to Joseph Dennie's *Port Folio* concluded that Hume "is often loose and careless in construction; and though he is unquestionably a graceful and an elegant writer, and, perhaps, unrivalled in the clearness and fluency of his narrative;

yet in dignity, in strength, in harmony and in purity, he is surpassed by Robertson, who in his History of Scotland, his first and, in our opinion, his happiest production, has exhibited a model of English composition superior to the style of any of his countrymen."[41] Another contributor to the same journal some years later made quite the opposite conclusion: "The general superiority of Hume over his rival is settled into a tranquil undisturbed sentiment, without any detraction from the genius and talents of Robertson."[42]

Comparisons between the two were usually between Hume's *History of England* and Robertson's *History of Scotland*, but Robertson was better known in the United States for his *History of America*, a work Poe borrowed from the University of Virginia library in August.[43] Poe withdrew other historical works from the library around the same time. William Wertenbaker, fellow student and then librarian, later recalled Poe perusing the collection "in search of old French books, principally histories."[44] In June, Poe borrowed three volumes of Charles Rollin's *Histoire ancienne* which treated early Egyptian, Carthaginian, Persian, and Grecian civilizations. Later in the summer, he borrowed two volumes of Rollin's *Histoire romaine*, both of which treated Caesar's Gallic Wars and the last years of the Roman Republic.[45] Near the end of August, he borrowed the first two volumes of John Marshall's *Life of George Washington*. Though nominally a biography, Marshall's narrative starts well before Washington's birth. The entire first volume, in fact, is a history of early America *before* Washington. Borrowing the earlier volumes of Marshall and not the later ones, Poe revealed his interest as American history in general, not necessarily the life of Washington.

Of all these various histories, only Rollin's directly concerned his schoolwork. Professor Long likely assigned Rollin for supplementary study. Sharing his attitude with Thomas Jefferson, Long firmly believed that the history and geography of a people should be studied with its language.[46] Reading the two works by Rollin, Poe not only learned about classical history, he also practiced reading French. The other histories he read, however, were written in English and treated either Great Britain or North America. The evidence suggests that Poe was not merely or even primarily studying history. Rather, he appears more interested in *history-writing*. The anecdotes left by Poe's fellow students agree that he had already begun to express his literary ambitions by writing poetry and critiquing the work of established writers. Might Poe's literary aspirations have allowed him to consider a career as a historian? "The perfect composition, the nervous language, the well-turned periods of Dr. Robertson inflamed me to the ambitious hope that I might one day tread in his footsteps: the calm philosophy, the careless inimitable beauties, of his friend and rival [Hume], often forced me to close the volume with a mixed sensation of delight and despair." The words are Gibbon's, as quoted in the *Port Folio*, but they might just as easily apply to any young man engaged in reading the finest literature of an earlier generation and wondering, with good reason, whether his literary ambition and talent could carry him to such heights.[47] Poe's unfulfilled desire to write a critical history of American literature can be traced back to his history reading at the University of Virginia.

By the third week of September, Poe had learned that he would be examined in both Ancient and Modern Languages during the last two weeks of the term. "The whole college has been put in great consternation by the prospect of an examination," he wrote to John Allan – "There is to be a general one on the first of December, which will occupy the time of the students till the fifteenth – the time for breaking up." Poe expressed the unfairness of those, like himself, who had been at school for only one session having to be examined with the second-year students, but resigned himself to the testing system and told Allan in the same letter, "I have been studying a great deal in order to be prepared, and dare say I shall come off as well as the rest of them."[48]

Also in the same letter, Poe boasted about the University of Virginia's excellent library, which had recently been moved from its temporary location to the Rotunda: "They have nearly finished the Rotunda – The pillars of the Portico are completed and it greatly improves the appearance of the whole – The books are removed into the library – and we have a very fine collection."[49] Poe would use the collection to further his study of French. In the first week of November, he withdrew both volumes of Nicolas Gouin Dufief's *Nature Displayed in Her Mode of Teaching Language to Man*.[50] His use of Dufief validates his statement to Allan that he was studying for his examination, but the work also reveals Poe's rebellion against his French teacher. Professor Blaetterman's European training gave him a traditional approach to teaching languages which was firmly grounded in the teaching of grammar. Dufief's approach to learning and teaching languages differed significantly from traditional pedagogy. Blaetterman was not responsible for the library's copy of Dufief. Like nearly all of the books then in the library, it had been placed there by the University's founder, Thomas Jefferson. Besides his pedagogical activities, Dufief sold books for a living, and Jefferson had frequented his Philadelphia shop. Dufief's work held special meaning for Jefferson, for, during his presidency, Jefferson had encouraged him to write it: "You will render a good service if you can abridge the acquisition of a new language."[51]

Essentially, Dufief applied Romanticism to pedagogy. Instead of learning grammatical rules, students of Dufief learned French according to Nature, that is, the same way a native speaker learns French as a child growing up. Dufief emphasized the importance of rote memorization of basic words and phrases. Much of the first volume of *Nature Displayed* is taken up by lists of nouns, grouped and ordered in much the same way a child growing up would first encounter such words. The first section contains nouns relating to such basic human needs as food, clothing, and shelter. Each noun is listed with a complete sentence using the word and a corresponding English translation of the word and the sentence. Subsequent lists of nouns expand the reader's spatial universe. The second section lists nouns describing urban surroundings. The third section includes words describing travel and the countryside; and the fourth section describes other countries and even other planets. Additional sections in the first volume treat pronouns, articles, adjectives, and adverbs. Dufief does not treat verb conjugation and syntax until well into the second volume.

By the time Poe read the work, Dufief's method had achieved a fair degree of acceptance in both the United States and England. First published in 1804, it went through its third edition in 1810. The following year, a Spanish textbook following Dufief's method was published at Philadelphia. Both the French and Spanish versions were reprinted in London that decade. Despite growing acceptance, Dufief's method had not influenced European methods of teaching language. When Poe borrowed the University of Virginia's copy of the fourth edition of *Nature Displayed* (1821), he challenged his teacher's pedagogical approach. Later remarks confirm Poe's commitment to the kind of approach Dufief recommended. Advising Frederick W. Thomas, one of his most loyal and sympathetic correspondents, how to study French, Poe wrote, "The best advice I can give you, under the circumstances, is to busy yourself with the theory or grammar of the language as little as possible and to read *side-by-side* translations continually, of which there are many to be found. I mean French books in which the literal English version is annexed page per page."[52] Fénelon's *Les aventures de Télémaque*, which Poe would later mention among important works of didactic fiction, had been the most popular French book in early America and remained so in Poe's day.[53] Elizabeth Ellis, daughter of John Allan's business partner, boasted about learning the work by heart.[54] Parallel English and French texts of *Les aventures de Télémaque* were widely available. In a follow-up letter to Thomas, Poe reinforced his earlier advice: "As regards the French – get into a French family by all means – read much, write more, and give grammar to the dogs."[55]

Poe may also have made a kind of parallel text for himself to facilitate his study of French at the University. Shortly after arriving, he had John Allan send him a copy of Alain René Le Sage's *History and Adventures of Gil Blas*, probably Tobias Smollett's English translation. Allan sent the volume begrudgingly, thinking that Poe was wasting time reading such frivolities, but Poe may have had more pragmatic reasons for rereading *Gil Blas*. Though he would later disparage the work's episodic quality, Poe had read *Gil Blas* in his youth, and his youthful impressions of the book's robbers and their secret cavern long occupied a place in his memory.[56] With the familiar English text nearby, Poe could have reread *Gil Blas* in French easily. What John Allan took for frivolity may have been another instance of Poe's scholarly devotion.

On 15 December, the University of Virginia faculty met. Professor Blaetterman reported Poe's name among the students "who excelled in the Senior French Class."[57] Less than a week later Poe, with no money to continue his schooling or pay his gambling debts, left the University.

When John Allan sent Poe the copy of *Gil Blas*, he bundled it with the two-volume *Cambridge Mathematics*, thus providing a practical textbook to counterbalance a seemingly frivolous piece of fiction. Poe received the package as a slap in the face. He had not registered for the mathematics course because Allan had not provided enough money to cover its cost. Poe believed a broad education was important and felt that mathematics would have enhanced his overall education significantly. He later applauded the educational plan of Thomas R. Dew, President of William and Mary College: "The plan embraces a course of general study which may be pursued to great advantage by all, without reference to the nature of the profession contemplated . . . For a degree in the classical department it is necessary that the candidate should not only be a proficient in the [grammatical] studies just mentioned, but that he should obtain a certificate of qualification on the junior mathematical, rhetorical and historical courses."[58] Mathematics would later become an important aspect of Poe's critical and aesthetic theory. As Padraic Colum has observed, "Poe's mentality was a rare synthesis: he had elements in him that corresponded with the indefiniteness of music and the exactitude of mathematics."[59] Disappointed and embittered by Allan's lack of financial support, Poe returned to his Richmond home where, unsurprisingly, the two quarreled. Within a few months Poe moved into separate lodgings and left the city shortly thereafter.

After leaving Allan's home, Poe wrote to him asking for passage money to Boston. Allan refused, castigating Poe for his desultory reading and his apparent inability to concentrate on his studies. Allan had no idea that besides fulfilling his required coursework in languages, Poe had been teaching himself British historiography on the side. In his letter refusing to give Poe the passage money, Allan wrote:

I taught you to aspire, even to eminence in Public Life, but I never expected that Don Quixotte, Gil Blas, Jo: Miller and such works were calculated to promote the end . . . the charge of eating the Bread of idleness, was to urge you to perseverance and industry in receiving the classics, in perfecting yourself in the mathematics, mastering the French.[60]

Allan's association of *Don Quixote* and *Gil Blas* is unsurprising. Le Sage's debt to Cervantes was well known, and the two works were often linked together. Smollett had translated both. (Poe later critiqued Smollett's translation of *Don Quixote* for its "extreme fastidiousness."[61]) One contemporary writer, however, thought each appealed to different readers, for "literary men are most delighted with Don Quixote, and men of the world with Gil Blas."[62] Linking the two books with *Joe Miller's Jests*, a jestbook popular for so long that the name of its titular author had become proverbial, Allan further stressed his belief that Poe was wasting his time with frivolities.

John Allan's references to *Don Quixote* and *Joe Miller's Jests* may

indicate books Poe had been reading after he left the University of
Virginia and returned to Allan's Richmond home. It hardly seems
unusual that Poe was indulging himself in pleasure reading. Besides
Joe Miller, Poe may have been reading another, even older collection
of humorous anecdotes, the *Gesta Romanorum*, a Latin work which
had had a significant influence on medieval and Renaissance authors
and which had recently appeared in a new English translation.[63]
Reviewing another jestbook, Poe commented, "Never was there a
better thing for whiling away a few loose or unappropriated half
hours – that is to say in the hands of a reader who is, even in a
moderate degree, imbued with a love of classical whimsicalities."[64]
Many serious college students who devote themselves to the study of
languages indulge in desultory reading once the school year is over.
Poe's predicament was worse than that of the usual undergraduate,
however, for he would not be returning to school when the next
session started in February. Poe never forgave Allan for denying him
an education: "A collegiate Education . . . was what I most ardently
desired, and I had been led to expect that it would at some future
time be granted – but in a moment of caprice – you have blasted my
hope."

CHAPTER 2

Poetry in manuscript and print

Though an angel should write, still 'tis devils must print.
    – Thomas Moore, "The Fudges in England"

After Edgar Allan Poe left John Allan's Richmond home in 1827, he made his way to Boston, enlisted in the US Army under the alias Edgar A. Perry, and published his first book of verse, *Tamerlane and Other Poems*, under the pseudonym, "A Bostonian." The first act, returning to Boston, appears motivated by Poe's wish to put some distance between himself and John Allan. His enlistment in the army seems less motivated by any patriotic desire to serve his country and more by basic human needs for food, shelter and clothing, the alias a way to mask his embarrassment. Poe's reasons for publishing a pseudonymous collection of verse are more complex. At the simplest level, his pseudonym, "A Bostonian," verifies his desire to distance himself from Allan and from Virginia. Never again would Poe so strongly identify with the city of his birth as he does on *Tamerlane*'s title page. Later, he derisively called Boston "Frogpondium" and once wrote, "We were born there – and perhaps it is just as well not to mention that we are heartily ashamed of the fact."[1] The act of publishing a collection of verse – especially a jejune collection scarcely long enough for a book, published by an obscure publisher with little or no reputation and in so few copies that, aside from a notice or two in the Boston periodicals, it would completely escape the public's attention – suggests Poe's need to prove himself, to show Allan that he could accomplish something, that he was not a good-for-nothing who idled his time reading picaresque romances and stale jestbooks.

The publication of *Tamerlane and Other Poems* occurred as the relationship between manuscript and print culture was undergoing significant change. Among fellow students at the University of

Virginia and members of the Jefferson Literary Society, Poe helped perpetuate the long-standing aristocratic Southern tradition of writing manuscript verse. Together a small group of friends would read their personal compositions aloud or else they would read one another's manuscript verse silently. If a poet's listeners or readers found one they particularly liked, they might transcribe it into their commonplace books so they could have a copy. If they did not like what they heard, the poet was a close enough friend for them to feel comfortable critiquing him. The poems which form the *Tamerlane* volume likely went through such a process. Manuscript culture at the University of Virginia manifested itself in more public ways as well. Describing a local controversy, Poe wrote that "every pillar in the University was white with scratched paper."[2] Almost as soon as the pillars were erected, in other words, they became a prominent, public space where enemies could attack and counterattack one another using the written word in lieu of sabers or fisticuffs.

Poe's Charlottesville had little local print culture *per se*. A small weekly paper, the *Central Gazette*, had been established in 1820, but the paper was scarcely distinguishable from other weekly small-town papers of the time, hardly the thing to attract the attention of serious-minded University students who read British quarterlies for pleasure. Elsewhere in the United States, however, more and more newspaper presses were being established, and copy-hungry editors were encouraging young men and women with literary ambitions to submit the products of their pen to the local newspaper office where the verses would be set in type within the paper's columns. True, they might be relegated to the far inside column adjacent to the market reports, but they would be printed.

The proliferation of newspapers, and the opportunities for publishing poetry within daily and weekly newspapers and monthly magazines which started becoming widespread during the 1820s, significantly altered the relationship between writer and reader. Instead of small groups of close friends, entire communities, few of whom knew the poet personally, began reading anonymous or pseudonymous amateur verse. The shift from manuscript to print not only contributed to the broadening readership of amateur literary efforts, it also changed the status of the verse text. Since the intimate readership of manuscript verse allowed for suggestion and revision, manuscript poems may have never been the same twice, changing with each reading and most suggestions from the readers.

The act of printing, on the other hand, gave poetry a fixed quality manuscript verse never had. Paradoxically, newsprint also made poetry ephemeral. Though its printed format made it look permanent, the newspaper was a disposable commodity. Manuscript volumes were often kept and treasured, but, depending on its frequency, a newspaper became so much waste paper a day or a week after its publication.

One young poet who took advantage of the expanding opportunities the newspaper and periodical press offered was Henry Poe. Born two years before his brother Edgar, Henry also began publishing poetry in 1827. His verses appeared in a new Philadelphia weekly, the *Saturday Evening Post*, in January and February and later that year in the short-lived Baltimore newspaper, the *North American or, Weekly Journal of Politics, Science and Literature*. The fact that Henry Poe took advantage of the new opportunities for publishing poetry offered by the newspaper and periodical press further distinguishes Edgar Allan Poe's *book* of verse. While newspaper editors encouraged submissions from young poets, few book publishers actively sought collections of verse which would be published in small print runs with virtually no chance of turning a profit.

The *Tamerlane* volume itself provides some clues for understanding the reasons for its publication. Poe used two lines from William Cowper as his title-page epigraph:

> Young heads are giddy, and young hearts are warm,
> And make mistakes for manhood to reform.

This apologetic epigraph gives readers the impression that the verses contained within the volume are products of the poet's youth and lets them know that they should be read in that spirit. The preface furthers the idea. Poe began: "The greater part of the Poems which compose this little volume, were written in the year 1821–2, when the author had not completed his fourteenth year." Though some and perhaps many of the poems had their genesis in Poe's early teens, there can be little doubt that he had since polished and sharpened them. Passing them off as products of his youth, Poe used the epigraph as a safeguard, a way to distance himself from the work. Should the volume be poorly received, he had a ready-built excuse and, with the motto from Cowper, a ready-made apology. Some readers, however, felt that youthful verse should remain in manuscript. One reviewer of *The Raven and Other Poems*, a volume which partially reprinted the contents of *Tamerlane and Other Poems*, commented, " 'Poems written during youth' no matter by whom written, are best preserved for the eye of the writer. The public forget the *youth*, and dwell only on the positive merits or demerits of the writing."[3]

The second sentence of the *Tamerlane* preface explains that the poems contained within the volume "were of course not intended for publication; why they are now published concerns no one but himself." Poe's refusal to explain himself only makes us more curious. The preface supplies a few oblique suggestions as to why he decided to publish a volume of youthful poetry. Concerning the title poem, Poe stated, "In Tamerlane, he has endeavoured to expose the folly of even *risking* the best feelings of the heart at the shrine of Ambition." In light of the great disappointment Poe felt after his withdrawal from the University of Virginia the year before, the statement appears autobiographical. Deprived of his education, Poe's literary ambitions seemed shattered.

The final paragraph of the preface, on the other hand, suggests that the volume's author might yet fulfill his literary ambitions: "He will not say that he is indifferent as to the success of these Poems – it might stimulate him to other attempts – but he can safely assert that failure will not at all influence him in a resolution already adopted." This sentence provides the key to understanding Poe's publication of *Tamerlane and Other Poems*, a collection of verse "not intended for publication." A printed volume, regardless how jejune, said something neither manuscript nor newspaper verse did; it conveyed a sense of professionalism. A volume of verse provided a level of status only the best poets deserved. With *Tamerlane and Other Poems*, Poe declared that, regardless of its success or failure, he was resolved to embark on a literary career.

Poe had written other verses during his adolescence besides those which made it into the *Tamerlane* volume. His teacher, Joseph H. Clarke, remembered him writing "pieces addressed to the different little girls in Richmond."[4] After Poe began publishing his poetry, he continued to write verse for young women not intended for publication, usually in the form of autograph verses written in the albums of female friends. Writing album verse was a popular fashion during the nineteenth century. People, mostly young women, would have friends, poets, or other worthies they might meet inscribe verses into ornately decorated blank books. Like giftbooks, albums were often given as holiday presents. One of Poe's autograph poems, for example, survives among verses written by others in an album bound in red morocco and adorned with a gilt spine and gold and black stamping on its cover.[5]

At mid century, Herman Melville spoofed the writing of ladies' album verse in *Pierre: Or, The Ambiguities*. Written after Poe's death, Melville's humorous remarks nevertheless provide useful insights into album verse-writing and therefore help us understand Poe's. In *Pierre*, Melville's title character becomes a famous juvenile author and must face the daunting task of writing multiple album verses, a task his procrastination makes all the more daunting. Many ladies' albums, whose "combined ornate bindings" dazzle his eyes, fill Pierre's bookshelf:

> The simplest of all things it is to write in a lady's album. But Cui Bono? Is there such a dearth of printed reading, that the monkish times must be revived, and ladies books be in manuscript? What could Pierre write of his own on Love or any thing else, that would surpass what divine Hafiz wrote so many long centuries ago? Was there not Anacreon too, and Catullus, and Ovid – all translated, and readily accessible? And then – bless all their souls! – had the dear creatures forgotten Tom Moore? But the handwriting, Pierre, – they want the sight of your hand.[6]

Pierre's thoughts suggest that in a world of print the act of circulating manuscripts was anachronistic and that contemporary verse could scarcely surpass the poetry of previous centuries. Ultimately, however, he understands that manuscript verse has a personal quality printed verse cannot possibly possess. Printed poetry and manuscript verse could coexist, for both fulfilled different purposes. Poe seems to have made a similar conclusion, though his precise thoughts on the subject have gone unrecorded. Pierre's predicament enlightens Poe's composition of album verse in another way. Poe's editors have often assumed that his album verses were impromptu compositions, written on request the moment a woman asked him. Album owners, as *Pierre* indicates, were willing to entrust their prized volumes to a poet's care long enough for him to write a thoughtful and heartfelt composition. This act of trust enhanced the personal relationship between album owner and poet.

Pierre also suggests that love was the proper theme for ladies' album verse, but surviving nineteenth-century albums show that poets had more latitude with their choice of subjects. Some of the poems express good wishes. Others belong to the remember-me-when-I-am-gone sort. Many offered pious reflections. And some provide philosophical reflections. Most express friendship. Nearly all exude sentimentalism.[7]

On 1 January, 1827, Miss Margaret Bassett received an album from her father as a New Year's gift, and she soon kept friends and acquaintances busy filling its blank leaves. The surviving manuscript volume contains Poe's earliest known album verse, "To Margaret." Where Melville would have Pierre respond to the ladies' albums by refusing to inscribe them and instead kissing them with "lipographs," Poe responded by writing an autograph verse which playfully derides the other verses inscribed within the volume. With "To Margaret" Poe both displayed his knowledge of English literary history and refuted the mediocre quality of the other poetry in Margaret Bassett's album. "To Margaret" is a cento or, in other words, a poem patched together from lines of well-known poetry. Here, however, Poe deliberately paraphrases classic lines to provide a commentary on the hackneyed verses within the album. The first two lines combine passages from Milton's *Paradise Lost* and Spenser's *Faerie Queene* to pose the question: "Who hath seduced thee to this foul revolt / From the pure well of Beauty undefiled?" Poe further deprecated the album's other manuscript verses in the next two lines, paraphrasing a passage from Cowper's *The Task:* "So banished from true wisdom to prefer / Such squalid wit to honourable rhyme?" Two Shakespeare plays, *Hamlet* and *Troilus and Cressida*, inspired the two lines which follow: "To write? To scribble? Nonsense and no more? / I will not write upon this argument." (Troilus had said to Pandarus: "I cannot fight upon this argument.") Pope's *Essay on Criticism* provided the basis for Poe's final line: "To write is human – not to write divine."[8] Poe's refusal to write album verse anticipates Pierre's, yet Poe's is ironic, for it occurs at the close of a poem he has just written. Such refusals, however, were also part of album verse-writing. One traditional verse exclaims:

> What! write in your album,
> For critics to spy,
> For the learned to laugh at?
> No, not I![9]

Album verse-writers often combined different passages from several traditional verses. Poe's cento parallels a poem assembled from several traditional lines, yet, by using literary sources instead of traditional lines, Poe removed the album verse from the realm of folklore into literary history.

"To Octavia," another of Poe's album verses, incorporates the traditional motifs of friendship and love. Instead of applauding friendship, however, the speaker of the poem conveys the inability of a convivial gathering of friends to make him forget his heart-throb Octavia. An autograph verse Poe left untitled, but which a posthumous editor labelled "Alone," further departs from the album-verse tradition. Instead of complimenting the album owner or expressing conviviality and friendship, the lines convey the poet's feelings of isolation. If "Alone" responds to other verses in the album, it does so by revealing the poet's inability to utter such popular effusions of sentimentality. The poem's confessional quality, however, may help it function as an album verse, for the loneliness evokes sympathy and provides a sense of intimacy between the poet and the female album owner and therefore strengthens their friendship.

Two of Poe's album verses, both written for Elizabeth Rebecca Harding, are acrostics, a genre of poetry with a greater affinity to a different tradition, the valentine. (Years later, Poe would lift the form to a higher level with his cross-acrostic, "A Valentine," written for Frances Sargent Osgood.) More than Poe's other autograph poetry, these two acrostics capture the spirit of traditional album verse, for they explicitly convey the tender feelings the poet has for the album owner.

Poe did not include his album poetry in his printed collections of verse. Poe scholars have generally concluded that Poe felt that their quality did not warrant publication. Discussing "Alone," I. B. Cauthen, for example, asserted that Poe was not proud enough of the poem to include it within his published volumes of poetry.[10] Poe chose not to print these poems not because of their quality; rather, he did not print them because they belonged to the manuscript tradition. In other words, Poe did not publish them because they were not intended as public documents. The work of Donald Reiman is useful for understanding the distinction. In his fine study of modern manuscripts, Reiman distinguishes three basic types: private manuscripts intended for a single individual; confidential manuscripts often addressed to an individual but shared among members of such close-knit groups as family, friends, or co-workers;

and public documents intended for dissemination to a wider readership.[11] Poe well understood the relationship between his writing and its intended readership. Album verses, as Poe realized, were confidential manuscripts written for the album owner and a handful of her close associates with whom she might share the album. Furthermore, confidential manuscript verse could be used as social capital. Some well-turned lines inscribed in a neat hand within the pages of a young lady's album, after all, could help secure her favor and allow the poet to enter her intimate circle of friends.

Young women were not the only ones with whom Poe used manuscript verse as social capital. After he finished writing "Al Aaraaf," yet before he published it, he showed the manuscript to William Wirt and sought his advice. Wirt had a reputation as Baltimore's grand old man of letters, and *Letters of the British Spy*, the work which had established his literary reputation a quarter of a century before, had gone through many subsequent editions since and remained in print. Despite Wirt's high literary reputation, Poe probably expected little worthwhile advice from him. Not only was Wirt's famous work decades old, it was patterned after a centuries-old work which had been popular in colonial America, Giovanni Paolo Marana's *Letters Writ by a Turkish Spy*.[12] Wirt responded to "Al Aaraaf" predictably:

I am sensible of the compliment you pay me in submitting it to my judgment and only regret that you have not a better counsellor. But the truth is that having never written poetry myself, nor read much poetry for many years, I consider myself as by no means a competent judge [of] poems. This is no doubt an old-fashioned idea resulting from the causes I have mentioned, my ignorance of modern poetry and modern taste. You perceive therefore that I am not qualified to judge of the merits of your poem. It will, I know, please modern readers – the notes contain a good deal of curious and useful information – but to deal candidly with you (as I am bound to do) I should doubt whether the poem will take with old-fashioned readers like myself. But this will be of little consequence – provided it be popular with modern readers – and of this, as I have already said, I am unqualified to judge.[13]

If Poe had expected any constructive criticism from Wirt, he would have been disappointed with these virtually meaningless remarks. Yet Poe's main intent, I believe, was simply to ingratiate himself to Wirt, a man who could help him get into West Point and who also could help expand his literary contacts. Wirt recommended other members of the literary community better able to further Poe's writing career, including Philadelphian Robert Walsh, the editor of the *American Quarterly Review* who was known as the "American Gentleman."[14] Poe soon sought Walsh's advice concerning "Al Aaraaf." Though it turned out to be disappointing, Poe's contact with Walsh allowed him to broaden his literary network to include the Philadelphia area.

Poe wrote to John Allan, informing him that he had personally introduced himself to William Wirt and asserting that his "first attempt at self introduction succeeded wonderfully – He treated me with great politeness, and invited me to call and see him frequently while I stay in Baltimore – I have called upon him several times."[15] When John Allan discovered that Poe had introduced himself to William Wirt, he was furious. Allan wrote to Poe "strongly censuring his conduct."[16] The precise reasons for Allan's angry response are not totally clear, yet it seems to originate with Poe's breach of etiquette. A person simply did not introduce himself to anyone, especially not to one of the most well-respected citizens in town. Not only was it bad manners for a person to introduce himself personally, it was also inappropriate for people to introduce themselves in writing. According to the rules of conduct, a mutual acquaintance should write a letter of introduction first.

After travelling to Philadelphia to meet Walsh, Poe attempted another self-introduction by writing to Philadelphia publisher Isaac Lea. Starting the letter, Poe admitted his breach in etiquette: "I should have presumed upon the politeness of Mr R. Walsh for a personal introduction to yourself, but was prevented by his leaving town the morning after my arrival – You will be so kind as to consider this as a *literary* introduction until his return from N. Y." He then provided a poem within the text of his letter:

> It was my choice or chance or curse
> To adopt the cause for better or worse
> And with my worldly goods and wit
> And soul and body worship it.[17]

In this letter, manuscript verse again functions as social capital. As album verses heighten the relationship between poet and album owner, this manuscript poem softens the impropriety of Poe's self-introduction and creates an intimacy between poet and publisher. These four lines paraphrase what Poe had expressed in the preface to *Tamerlane*, the idea that he was ready to devote his heart and soul to poetry. Evoking the language of the marriage ceremony, Poe made his relationship to poetry a sacred union never to be broken. The purpose of the letter was to convince Lea to consider "Al Aaraaf" for publication. Poe's self-introduction apparently worked, for he soon met Isaac Lea who agreed to publish "Al Aaraaf" – providing Poe would guarantee the book against any loss. John Allan, however, refused to put up the money, so Poe did not publish "Al Aaraaf" in Philadelphia.

At West Point the following year, Poe continued to use manuscript verse as social capital. He was older than most of the cadets, so they naturally looked up to him, but his satirical lines about the instructors and officers at the military academy really endeared him to his fellow cadets. One of them, Thomas W. Gibson, recalled that almost daily Poe issued "poems and squibs of local interest," which quickly circulated through the classes. Joseph Locke, who Gibson described as "one of the instructors of tactics, and *ex-officio* Inspector of Barracks, and supervisor of the morals and deportment of cadets generally," was Poe's favorite satiric target.[18] Another cadet stated that Poe "would often write some of the most forcible and vicious doggerel, have me copy it with my left hand in order that it might be disguised, and post it around the building."[19] So displayed, Poe's satiric verses recall the manuscript attacks his fellow students posted on the columns at the University of Virginia.

By all accounts, Poe wrote numerous verse satires at West Point, yet only one survives:

> As for Locke, he is all in my eye,
>   May the d—l right soon for his soul call.
> He never was known to lie –
>   In bed at a *reveillé* "roll call."

> John Locke was a notable name;
>   Joe Locke is a greater; in short,
> The former was well known to fame,
>   But the latter's well known "to report."[20]

More than anything else, Poe's skill at versifying established his reputation at West Point. When he proposed a published collection of verse, "great expectations," another cadet remembered, "were formed of the book," and well over half of them subscribed to *Poems*.[21] The numerous subscriptions testify to Poe's personal charisma as well as the popularity of his manuscript verse. Lacking Poe's literary sophistication, however, the cadets assumed that the printed volume would be a collection of the satirical verses Poe had written during his time at West Point. When they saw the volume, they felt cheated. Not only was it poorly printed on cheap paper, but, even worse, it contained *none* of the satirical verses which had so endeared them to Poe.

The cadets' disappointment came from their failure to understand what Poe well knew: that manuscript poetry circulated among a group of young men who shared the same lifestyle and many of the same beliefs was not necessarily suitable for print. Besides ingratiating him to his fellow cadets, Poe's verse satires served to vent his frustration with the rigid military discipline. The feelings Poe turned into rhyme were shared by many of the others and made them recognize in Poe a kindred spirit. The poetical lampoons of Joe Locke and company, if published, would not retain the significance they had among Poe's fellow cadets. Read by those who did not share their insiders' view of cadet life, the poems, though clever, would seem little more than petty vindictiveness. As a young man, Poe understood that personal satire, like album verses written for young women, belonged to the manuscript tradition.

Since Poe's fellow cadets did not recognize how inappropriate it would have been for him to have published his satirical jibes, he greatly sank in their estimation after *Poems* appeared. Gibson recalled, "For months afterward quotations from Poe formed the standing material for jests in the corps, and his reputation for genius went down at once to zero."[22] Gibson's remark indicates that Poe himself became the object of verse satire after *Poems* appeared. His printed verses entered West Point's oral culture, not as he wrote them, but in the form of verse parodies.

After leaving West Point, Poe made his way back to Baltimore where he continued writing poetry and, partially inspired by the financial opportunities writing contests offered, began writing tales. Poe's contest submissions will be treated in greater detail in the following chapter, yet one aspect of them is relevant here: the physical appearance of the manuscript he submitted to the Baltimore *Saturday Visiter* contest. John H. B. Latrobe, one of the judges, remembered the manuscript's appearance well. Years later he described it as "a small quarto bound book that had, until then, accidentally escaped attention, possibly because so unlike, externally, the bundles of manuscript that it was to compete with . . . Instead of the common cursive manuscript, the writing was in Roman characters – an imitation of printing."[23] The numerous examples of Poe's manuscript verse show that he clearly understood the distinction between manuscript and print culture and recognized the propriety of each. Unlike his other manuscript verse, however, the *Visiter* submission was not intended as a confidential manuscript. It was submitted with the hope that it would win the contest and be published within the magazine's pages. Surviving Poe manuscripts indicate that his fair-copy submissions to editors and publishers were often in Roman characters instead of cursive. In other words, Poe used cursive writing for his private and confidential manuscripts; he used Roman characters for his public documents.

As a handwritten document made to resemble the printed word, Poe's submission to the *Saturday Visiter* contest blurred the boundaries between print and manuscript culture. When he later became professionally associated with the periodical press, he continued to challenge the distinctions between print and manuscript. In the *Southern Literary Messenger*, Poe included a two-part article called "Autography" which printed and analyzed facsimiles of autographs from prominent American authors. With "Autography" Poe deliberately conflated manuscript and print, confidential and public. Except for playwrights and orators, professional authors in Poe's day portrayed themselves to the public through the medium of print. The autograph, on the other hand, belonged to the manuscript culture. Printing personal autographs, Poe made a private or confidential manuscript public. Analyzing them, Poe offered insights into authors' characters which readers might not have discerned from their printed works. Thus, he used the printed page to provide his readers with a reading experience analogous to personal contact.

Poe's later "Marginalia" series similarly blurred manuscript and print. Marginalia, after all, were highly personal comments; Baudelaire characterized Poe's "Marginalia" as the secret chambers of his mind.[24] In an annotated volume, the margins are the place where reader and text meet and, for that matter, where manuscript and print culture come together. Inscribing the margins of a book, the bookowner makes the volume his own. Separately publishing one's personal marginalia presented a problem, however, for it involved separating manuscript from printed text. In other words, it took texts not meant to stand alone and stood them alone. Poe explicitly acknowledged the problem: "The main difficulty respected the mode of transferring the notes from the volumes – the context from the text – without detriment to that exceedingly frail fabric of intelligibility in which the context was imbedded."[25] For Poe, of course, the problem was one in theory only. Since the texts he presented as his marginalia were largely fictional inventions, any apparent loss of context was deliberate. The separate publication of one's marginalia within the columns of a magazine further complicates the relationship between manuscript and print culture. While marginal notes are private manuscripts, the act of gathering them into a magazine column makes them public. Poe's "Marginalia" implies that the observations made by an astute bookman during the course of his solitary reading warranted recognition. Private genius deserved public attention.

One more example by way of conclusion: when Poe was looking for support for the *Broadway Journal* in 1845, he wrote an autograph letter and had a woodcut of it made and printed in multiple copies to distribute to potential subscribers and financial backers. In so doing, Poe gave a printed document the aura of a manuscript. Though Edgar Allan Poe recognized print media as the cultural location where he would make his fame, he never forgot the literary traditions belonging to the manuscript culture. His use of manuscript material after he started publishing reveals his shrewd efforts to blur the boundaries between private and public. It is no coincidence that he decided to title his ideal magazine the *Stylus*.

CHAPTER 3

Baltimore book culture

Read, at a stall (for oft one pops
On something at these stalls and shops,
That does to quote, and gives one's Book
A classical and knowing look. –
Indeed I've found, in Latin, lately,
A course of stalls improves me greatly)
    – Thomas Moore, "The Fudge Family in Paris"

In mid-1829, a time after he had received his discharge from the army yet before he had been accepted to West Point, Edgar Allan Poe was living in Baltimore with virtually no money and little else but the clothes on his back. In the second week of August he wrote to John Allan with a request: "I left behind me in Richmond a small trunk containing books and some letters – will you forward it on to Baltimore to the care of *H-W. Bool Jr* and if you think I may ask so much perhaps you will put in it for me some few clothes as I am nearly without." Henry W. Bool, Jr., was a book dealer who had been living and working in Baltimore for many years. A mutual acquaintance recalled, "He was a Northern man, and settled in Baltimore in the capacity of vendor of second-hand books. His *magasin* was a cellar, and his assortment of mutilated *tomes* elicited much attention on the part of the antiquarian book-worm."[1]

Since coming to Baltimore in or before 1820, Bool had actively engaged in many aspects of the book trade. He had served as a subscription book agent, book auctioneer, proprietor of the Cheap Book Store, proprietor of the Repository of Cheap Books, and new book auction and commission merchant.[2] The year Poe came to know him he tried his hand at publishing with *The Patriotic Sailor: Or, Sketches of the Humors, Cares, and Adventures of a Naval Life*, an anonymous, two-volume sea novel published at Bool's "Cheap Repository, No. 60 Baltimore Street," which may have partially inspired Poe's *Narrative of Arthur Gordon Pym*. Bool's "eccentricities made him a noted character," and his Baltimore Street salesroom developed a reputation as "the lounging place of all the wags in the city" where many "humorous scenes took place."[3] There can be little doubt that the opportunity to read, loiter, and discuss books attracted Poe during his drifter's days, but the bookish opportunities Bool offered may not have been the only or even the primary reason Poe made his acquaintance, for, among his other business ventures, Bool also ran an intelligence office, the nineteenth-century equivalent of the modern-day employment agency. Poe was looking for a job.

No documentary evidence survives to show whether or not Henry Bool found Poe a job in 1829, but his decade-long experience in the book business allowed him to give Poe valuable advice for later use. Within a year, Poe had reached West Point, and within another year after that he had been court-martialed and dismissed. Before leaving, however, Poe solicited enough subscriptions among the cadets to finance *Poems*, his third collection of verse. Bool's experience as a subscription book agent offered Poe the know-how for publishing *Poems* by subscription, which, after all, was really quite shrewd. At the time, anyone publishing a book by subscription generally had to pay a percentage to the agent who solicited the subscriptions and another percentage to the one who collected the money.[4] Poe avoided the first by soliciting subscriptions himself, and he avoided the second by having the US Army collect the money for him. In the first half of 1831, Poe returned to Baltimore. He moved in with his paternal aunt, Maria Clemm, and her daughter Virginia. He likely recontacted Henry Bool, still doing business at 60 Baltimore Street, for Poe once more needed a job and a place to read and loiter.

Bool's, of course, was not the only place a young man who took an interest in literature could while away time in Baltimore during the early 1830s. Far from it. Baltimore had a lively book culture and many bookdealers. Edward J. Coale, for instance, had been retailing books in Baltimore for over two decades, and his store on Calvert Street has long been considered one of Poe's haunts.[5] Another acquaintance of Poe's remembered Coale for his kindness, his usefulness, and his good heart.[6] The fact that Poe had his manuscript volume of tales finely bound for the *Saturday Visiter* contest suggests that his contacts among Baltimore bookmen extended to bookbinders as well, including one who was friendly enough to bind a manuscript volume gratis.

Bookdealers less accommodating than Bool or less kind-hearted than Coale may have been reluctant to allow a down-and-out young man to dawdle within their doors for long periods of time, but some contemporary booksellers offered an economical alternative to purchasing books: the circulating library. Many dealers kept a shelf or two of books from which customers could borrow volumes for as little as a few pennies a week. While most circulating libraries consisted of little else but popular sentimental novels, some booksellers allowed regular stock that did not sell readily to be circulated. Others brought the circulating library to a new level of sophistication. None were more successful in Baltimore than the printer–bookseller Joseph Robinson who had opened a circulating library by 1812 and literary rooms a half-dozen years later. The establishment contained four rooms. Two were downstairs: the book delivery room, which also served as the reception area, and the ladies' reading room, which contained reading tables, writing desks, and a pianoforte. The two upstairs rooms were for the men, a quiet room for study and book-reading and another for conversation and newspaper-reading. Distinguishing book-reading from newspaper-reading and associating newspaper-reading with conversation, the arrangement of Robinson's literary rooms provides an important insight into the reading process during the early nineteenth century. Access to such luxurious reading opportunities had a price, however. Library privileges at Robinson's cost six dollars a year and access to his literary rooms four dollars more. Poe may have never seen the inside of Robinson's circulating library, his poverty relegating him to those which charged by the book.[7]

The circulating libraries were commercial ventures, but Poe's Baltimore had other libraries which were social undertakings. To form these social libraries, groups of like-minded men and, occasionally, a few women would subscribe or, in other words, purchase shares entitling them to borrow volumes from the collection and to help decide which volumes the library would contain. Benjamin Franklin, who had given these library companies their start a hundred years before, retold the story in his *Autobiography*, copies of which were ubiquitous in Poe's time.[8] After the communal library planned by the members of Franklin's junto failed, Franklin and his friends formed the Library Company of Philadelphia in 1731, the

"Mother of all the North American Subscription Libraries," as he later called it.[9] Over the next century, the social or subscription library flourished. At first, only well-to-do gentlemen could afford to subscribe to the library companies, but by the early nineteenth century, groups of other like-minded people began forming social libraries often named for the shared interests of their subscribers. Mercantile and mechanics' libraries flourished. Baltimore had at least two subscription libraries during the early 1830s: the Library Company of Baltimore and the Apprentices' Library.

First established in 1795, the Library Company of Baltimore attracted the city's gentlemen, members of the professional classes, and successful merchants who were willing and able to purchase a share in the company and pay annual dues. At the time Poe lived in Baltimore, shares cost fifty dollars and annual fees five or ten dollars. Poe could not have afforded to join the Library Company of Baltimore, but his second cousin Neilson Poe was a member when Poe came to Baltimore, and would have been able, though not necessarily willing, to withdraw books for Edgar Poe's use.[10] The finest library in the city, the Library Company of Baltimore had a diverse collection which included theology and ecclesiastical history; moral philosophy; arts and sciences; law and politics; trade and commerce; history and biography; voyages and travels; and a good belletristic collection containing such important aesthetic works as Isaac Disraeli's *Essay on the Manners and Genius of Literary Characters*, Alexander Gerard's *Essay on Taste* as well as his *Essay on Genius*, William Smith's edition of Longinus, Lord Kames's *Elements of Criticism*, and Madame de Stael's *Influence of Literature upon Society* as well as her *Germany, being Essays upon the Manners and Literature of the Germans*. Poetry titles included Wordsworth's and Coleridge's *Lyrical Ballads* and Lord Byron's *Childe Harold, Corsair,* and *English Bards and Scotch Reviewers*, a satire Poe found coarse and malignant.[11]

When (or if) Neilson Poe was unwilling to borrow books for his cousin and when Edgar Poe lacked even the few pennies needed to borrow books from the circulating libraries, his only recourse was to return to those bookstores run by men like Bool and Coale who did not mind someone hanging around, reading and not spending money. Though Poe was a little out at the sleeves, he was no derelict. After all, he had already published three collections of verse. His volumes of poetry had not gained him the notoriety he had hoped for, but he could use their publication to reassure bookdealers that he was a serious writer, not just some vagrant seeking refuge from the cold.

At the new bookstores, Poe could have found a wide variety of books for sale. Besides the staples of the book trade – almanacs, spelling books, songbooks, conduct books, chapbooks, psalters, and catechisms – the Baltimore press issued numerous other books during the early 1830s. Giftbooks, including N. C. Brooks's *The Amethyst*, were becoming increasingly popular. Brooks devoted much effort to enhancing Baltimore's literary reputation, and he would become an associate of Poe's.[12] Giftbooks would become an important outlet for Poe's fiction. Some of his finest tales "William Wilson," "The Pit and the Pendulum," "The Purloined Letter" – would appear in giftbooks. His "Siope – A Fable" would appear in a local one, *The Baltimore Book*.[13] Yet another edition of William Wirt's *Letters of the British Spy* appeared in 1831. English translations of Plutarch's *Lives* and Josephus' *Works* were also published in Baltimore during the early 1830s. Several editions of Baron Munchausen's *Travels and Adventures* appeared, too. Books about the American West were gaining more attention. Mary Austin Holley's *Texas*, a work promoting Western emigration, and Philip L. Edwards's *Rocky Mountain Correspondence*, a travelogue, were both published in Baltimore. Frederick Marryat's *Peter Simple: Or, Adventures of a Midshipman* was reprinted in Baltimore in 1833. Though Poe disliked Marryat's work generally, he found "truthfulness, naturalness, and *bonhommie*" in *Peter Simple* and asserted that "no better nautical adventures are to be met with than we find in this the best of his novels."[14] Other fiction reprinted in Baltimore he found less agreeable. In 1834, Joseph Robinson reprinted William Beckford's *Vathek*, a work Poe called a "heterogenous, tumid, and blasphemous piece of *Easternism*."[15]

Besides the Baltimore imprints, the new bookstores would have stocked the latest publications from Boston, New York, and Philadelphia. Works published during the 1831–1834 period which Poe became familiar with include three by William Gilmore Simms: *Atalantis: A Story of the Sea*; *Martin Faber: The Story of a Criminal*; and *Guy Rivers: A Tale of Georgia*.[16] Seba Smith's *Life and Writings of Major Jack Downing of Downingsville Away Down East in the State of Maine*, a work Poe characterized as "coarse, but full of fun, wit, sarcasm, and sense," was also available.[17] A Philadelphia edition of Mary Shelley's *Frankenstein* appeared in 1833. Horace Wemyss Smith recalled Poe reading the work in Philadelphia some years later, which must be taken with some skepticism, for Smith's recollection is almost too good to be true. As he remembered it, Poe read *Frankenstein* while seated in the doorway of the Smith family mausoleum.[18] Edward Bulwer-Lytton's *Eugene Aram* and his *The Pilgrims of the Rhine* were reprinted in the United States during the early 1830s. Frances Trollope's often derogatory *Domestic Manners of the Americans* appeared around this time: a work that met with great disfavor among American readers who, as Poe recorded, joked that the book might have been better titled *Manners of the American Domestics*.[19] Several works influencing Poe's critical outlook were reprinted in the United States during the early 1830s: Charles Lamb's *Last Essays of Elia*, James Montgomery's *Lectures on General Literature*, and, most importantly, John Black's English translation of August Wilhelm von Schlegel's *Course of Lectures on Dramatic Art and Literature*, reprinted in Philadelphia in 1833. Some London imports were also available such as Thomas Carlyle's *Sartor Resartus*, a work Poe did not greatly appreciate. He later commented, "We will venture to bet that the meaning (if there be any) of the Sartor Resartus has only the two faults of the steed in Joe Miller. In the first place, it is hard to catch. In the second place it is worth nothing when caught."[20]

Personal contacts gave Poe further opportunity to become part of Baltimore book culture. To understand Baltimore's literary elite in Poe's day, we need to go back a decade and a half to mid-1816 when a group of professional men, mainly attorneys and physicians, many of whom were veterans of the War of 1812, gathered to form the Delphian Club, a literary coterie named after the oracle at Delphi and reminiscent of a similar gathering of Maryland's men of letters the century before, the Tuesday Club. Membership, the founders decided, would be limited to nine at any given time, allowing each to consort with a different muse. Its members included John Neal before he left Baltimore to sojourn in England and eventually to settle in Maine; William Gwynn, an old bachelor who "enjoyed a bottle of good wine with as much gusto as did John Falstaff his sack," characteristically sported "a high white cravat" with "his hair done up in a queue," and became the club's last president in 1824; and John H. B. Latrobe, the last member to join the club before it dissolved.[21] All members received club names. Neal, whose most famous written work was a poem on Niagara Falls, was known as

Jehu O'Cataract. Gwynn was known as Odopoeus Oligostichus for
his ability with epigrams, puzzles, and newspaper-squibs. At repartee, he was "quick and cutting, and an avalanche of anecdote
never failed to issue from his lips when at the festive board."[22]
Latrobe was alternatively known as Orlando Garangula, Choleric
Combustible, and Sir John Mittimus of Mittimus Hall. Neal later
characterized his fellow Delphians: "High-minded, generous, unsel-
fish men, they were both intellectual and companionable, indulgent,
and with all their whims and freaks, congenial."[23] Though membership was always limited to nine, non-members were welcome, and
many of Baltimore's prominent men of letters often attended.
Visitors included John P. Kennedy, Francis Scott Key, Rembrandt
Peale, and William Wirt. Many members and visitors contributed to
the *Red Book*, a Baltimore periodical published from 1816 to 1820
which served as the club's unofficial organ.

In its early years, the club met every Saturday evening, different
club members taking turns as host. In its last years, they began
meeting regularly at the home of William Gwynn, who lived in Bank
Lane near St. Paul Street in a residence known as Tusculum. Books
formed a prominent part of Tusculum's interior. John P. Kennedy
once described Gwynn's study as containing "the learned confusion
of plans, pamphlets, and commentaries – maps and globes – sketches
of the moon – scraps for the Red Book – strictures upon women –
Montaigne, Cervantes, and Sterne peering through the glasses of a
polished book case and contrasted with Bacon, Boyle, Locke, who
occupy an obscure recess on the other side."[24] The club officially
disbanded in late 1824 or 1825, but Gwynn remained the unofficial
head of Baltimore's literary elite, and Tusculum remained a gathering place for the city's men of letters. Gwynn extended his welcome
beyond the professional classes, and his home developed a reputation as "the headquarters of the literati, the artists, actors, and
Bohemians of the time," a reputation it continued to maintain when
Edgar Allan Poe first came to Baltimore in 1829.[25]

Poe introduced himself to William Wirt shortly after he arrived in
Baltimore, and he met William Gwynn not much later. Just a few
years younger than Wirt, Gwynn had more to offer Poe in practical
terms, for he was proprietor and editor of the *Federal Gazette and
Baltimore Daily Advertiser*. Though Poe had to introduce himself to
Wirt, he need not have had to introduce himself to Gwynn, for
Neilson Poe was on the *Federal Gazette* staff and could have intro-

duced his cousin. Gwynn had a reputation for an even temper, kindness, benevolence, and good advice. After Poe showed him a manuscript of "Al Aaraaf," Gwynn kept it long enough to read the poem and share it with a friend. Gwynn's reaction to the work, however, was much the same as Wirt's had been. It "was not in his vein."[26] Nevertheless, he would have encouraged the young poet to continue writing. Earlier Gwynn had encouraged both Neal and Latrobe to write books of their own.[27] Furthermore, Gwynn permitted an extract of "Al Aaraaf" to appear in the *Federal Gazette.* William Wirt had suggested other writers and journalists for Poe to meet; Gwynn had additional contacts. He may have given Poe his most important early literary contact, John Neal.

Poe's new connections among the Baltimore literati also may have helped him find a publisher for *Al Aaraaf, Tamerlane and Minor Poems.* The volume was published at the end of 1829 by Hatch and Dunning, Baltimore booksellers with little publishing experience. Earlier that year Hatch and Dunning had published an English translation of a French medical treatise, Jean Antoine Saissy's *Essay on the Diseases of the Internal Ear.* Since many of Gwynn's friends and Baltimore's most prominent literati were also the city's most important physicians, the same men who convinced Hatch and Dunning to publish the medical work could have encouraged the firm to publish a collection of avant-garde poetry. Indeed, the same logic could have been used to convince them to publish one as much as the other: "The book won't make any money, but it will enhance your prestige."

Returning to Baltimore in 1831, his West Point experience behind him, Poe renewed his acquaintances among the Baltimore literati. He wrote to William Gwynn, asking him for a job on his newspaper, now called the *Baltimore Gazette and Daily Advertiser.*[28] Neilson Poe had left Gwynn to become owner and editor of the *Frederick Examiner,* a semi-weekly paper in Frederick, Maryland. Edgar Poe hoped he might fill Neilson's position but told Gwynn that he was willing to work in any capacity. Gwynn doubted whether Poe would make a good employee, however. After reading "Al Aaraaf," Gwynn had confidentially spoken of the poem "as indicative of a tendency to anything but the business of matter of fact life."[29] The comment reveals a key difference between Poe's attitude toward literature and that of Gwynn and other Baltimore literati. For Poe, being a writer was an all-consuming endeavor, something requiring the devotion of heart, mind, and soul. For Gwynn, writing was a pleasant diversion, a leisurely activity to beguile the time. Being a man of letters was an avocation, not a vocation. Even the business of editing a newspaper was more hobby than anything else. John Neal wrote that during the 1820s nearly all of Baltimore's editors, "were proprietors, occasionals, or supernumeraries, often government-officials, leading politicians, and statesmen, who were glad to 'work for nothing, and find themselves.'"[30] Poe saw newspaper or magazine editing as a professional activity, yet it had not fully become one. In Baltimore during the early 1830s, editing was in a transition state between gentlemanly pursuit and professional endeavor.

The lives of two men in particular, who affected Poe while he lived in Baltimore during the early 1830s – John Hill Hewitt, whom Henry W. Bool facetiously called the "Byron of America," and Lambert A. Wilmer – help indicate the editor's uneasy place in the world of print culture.[31] Hewitt, a music teacher, devoted part of his time to editing, and contributing articles to, the *Baltimore Minerva and Emerald*, including a harsh review of *Al Aaraaf, Tamerlane, and Minor Poems*.[32] Wilmer, who had spent his early years in Baltimore, returned there in January 1832 to edit the *Baltimore Saturday Visiter*. The arrangement Wilmer had with this literary magazine's proprietor, Charles F. Cloud, marks a significant shift toward professional editing. Cloud invested the capital required for the venture while Wilmer invested his time and expertise to edit the magazine. Together they would share the profits equally. The arrangement worked well at first, and the *Baltimore Saturday Visiter* achieved a modest degree of success despite predictions of its quick demise by local nay-sayers.[33] Wilmer's life outside the editorial office was also quite pleasant. He and Poe became fast friends and spent much time together. "Almost every day," Wilmer subsequently recalled, "we took long walks in the rural districts near Baltimore, and had long conversations on a great variety of subjects."[34] Poe later paid tribute to his friend's literary skill: "Within a circle of *private* friends, whom Mr. Wilmer's talents and many virtues have attached devotedly to himself, and among whom we are very proud in being ranked, his writings have been long appreciated, and we sincerely hope the days are not far in futurity when he will occupy that full station in the *public* eye to which his merits so decidedly entitle him."[35]

The magazine Hewitt was associated with, the *Baltimore Minerva*, folded not long after the *Visiter* had begun, so Hewitt approached

C. F. Cloud and offered to edit the *Visiter* for nothing. Wilmer explained that Hewitt had "other means of maintenance besides authorship or editorial labor, and he therefore possessed the manifold advantages of such American writers as can afford to 'work for nothing and find themselves.'"[36] Cloud accepted Hewitt's offer and dismissed Wilmer who took the dismissal as a violation of their agreement. Wilmer subsequently filed suit and won. The judicial decision emphasized the increasing professionalization of editing, though it did little to advance Wilmer's career. Soured by the ordeal, he soon left Baltimore. Though Wilmer's experience shows that editing was in the process of becoming a professional endeavor, it had not advanced far enough in that direction to help Poe from his present circumstances. He still remained an outsider to Baltimore's periodical press.

With neither job nor prospect of one by the end of May 1832, Poe found the $100 prize that the Philadelphia *Saturday Courier* offered in a short-story contest an enticing opportunity. Contestants had six months before the December deadline. Poe spent much of that time writing, submitting at least five stories to the contest: "The Bargain Lost," an early version of "Bon-Bon;" "A Decided Loss," which he would later retitle "Loss of Breath"; "The Duke de L'Omelette"; "Metzengerstein"; and "A Tale of Jerusalem." Despite his efforts, he lost the contest to Delia S. Bacon who had already established herself as a writer and whose popular success would continue afterwards. Some years later, Poe had the opportunity to review one of her historical novels, *The Bride of Fort Edward*. The work was published anonymously, and Poe was unaware of the author's identity, so his comments hold no spite, only frankness. He remarked, "Nothing less than a long apprenticeship to letters will give the author . . . even a chance to be remembered or considered." In its minor points, Poe found *The Bride of Fort Edward* "radically deficient in all the ordinary and indispensable proprieties of literature" and concluded that the author's "prose stands sadly in need of a straight jacket."[37]

A year and a half later, still poor, still unable to find permanent employment, and still longing for literary fame, Poe entered another literary contest. When the *Baltimore Saturday Visiter*, now edited by Hewitt, announced their contest and prizes, they also listed the judges: John P. Kennedy, John H. B. Latrobe, and Dr. James H. Miller. As yet, Poe had not met any of these three, though he knew Kennedy from *Swallow Barn*, which had first appeared the preceding year. Reviewing a later Kennedy novel, Poe said, "We have not yet forgotten, nor is it likely we shall very soon forget, the rich simplicity of diction – the manliness of tone – the admirable traits of Virginian manners, and the striking pictures of still life, to be found in Swallow Barn."[38] Also, Poe may have heard about Kennedy's and Latrobe's association with the Delphian Club in conversation with William Gwynn or in correspondence with John Neal. Poe's likely knowledge of the Delphians makes it remarkable that he submitted his entries in a bound manuscript volume titled "Tales of the Folio Club," a collection which would have contained an early version of Poe's "Folio Club," a sketch which lampoons the Delphians.[39]

Humorous depictions of the Delphians were not unprecedented in fiction, however. John Neal had mentioned the club in his 1823 epistolary novel, *Randolph*. Having visited the Delphians the night before, one of Neal's fictional correspondents explains that "never was it my misfortune to see such a heap of intellectual rubbish and glitter, in all my life . . . They call themselves the *he*-muses. And each one has a companion allotted him from among the nine *she*-ones."[40] He then goes about describing individual club members and their various shenanigans. Though Neal made fun at the club's expense, his description of it is basically good-hearted.

Poe's "Folio Club" has a sharper edge, but it is not altogether derogatory. Though the tale criticizes the club's members and their attitudes toward literature, it also conveys the pleasure which comes when a group of well-to-do gentlemen gather for a night of conviviality and *bons mots*. Poe's Folio Club does recall Baltimore's Delphians, but his satire is more broadly cast. Calling the Folio Club "a mere Junto of *Dunderheadism*," Poe used a word associated with Benjamin Franklin whose junto was a group of young men who assembled for intellectual companionship. Though Poe described the separate members of the Folio Club, they do not correspond directly to the Delphians. Mr. Snap "formerly in the service of the Down-East Review" suggests Neal who was now living and working in Maine as editor of the *Yankee*,[41] but another member, "Mr. Blackwood Blackwood who had written certain articles for foreign Magazines," also recalls Neal who had contributed to *Blackwood's* during his sojourn in England. The "stout gentleman who admired Sir Walter Scott" could refer to William Gwynn whom Latrobe described as being "very fat" late in 1831.[42] Poe's satiric targets, however, were more general. He was attacking all stout gentlemen who admired Scott, not any particular one.

Most importantly, Poe criticized the old-fashioned ideas about literature the stout gentleman and his ilk held, specifically, the notion that literature must both delight and instruct. The avowed purpose of the club, after all, was the "instruction of society, and the amusement of themselves."[43] To fit his own tales embodying the aesthetic principles he had earlier articulated in the "Letter to B" prefacing the 1831 *Poems*, Poe had the club abandon their instructive function for the nonce and devote their evening of stories solely to their own amusement.

When Kennedy, Latrobe, and Miller gathered to decide the contest winners, their activity recalled the days of the Delphian Club. As Latrobe remembered, they met "one pleasant afternoon in October, 1833" in the back parlor of his home, sitting "around a table garnished with some old wine and some good cigars," and began their deliberations.[44] By the time they were through, Poe's "MS. in a Bottle" was chosen as the best short story, and "Song of the Winds," a poem Hewitt had submitted under the pseudonym "Henry Wilton," was awarded the first prize for poetry over the verses Poe had submitted.

When Poe learned that "Henry Wilton" was a pseudonym and that Hewitt, the editor of the magazine sponsoring the contest, had actually written the winning poem, he accosted Hewitt in the street, accusing him of winning the prize by underhanded means. Hewitt denied it. When Poe next asked why he had used a pseudonym, Hewitt answered the question vaguely: "I had my reasons." Poe insulted Hewitt, and Hewitt struck Poe. Luckily, passing friends stopped the quarrel before one man could challenge the other to a duel.[45] Later describing the *Baltimore Saturday Visiter* long after Hewitt had left the weekly magazine, Poe called it "a journal which has never yet been able to recover from the *mauvais odeur* imparted to it by Hewitt."[46]

Though the contest results spurred the heated conflict between the two men, their dispute reflects a larger issue, the idea of editorial professionalism. At the time he entered the contest, Hewitt was editor of the *Saturday Visiter*, yet he saw no conflict of interest. Since he was not being remunerated to edit the magazine, he felt free to enter a contest its owners were sponsoring. His entry did not seem unprofessional to Hewitt, for he did not consider himself a professional. Poe saw the matter differently. Regardless of whether Hewitt was getting paid or not, he was the editor and had the responsibility to act in a professional manner. Poe's reaction to Hewitt's behavior reveals the seriousness with which he regarded the literary profession, a seriousness all the more remarkable considering Poe had yet to work in any editorial capacity.

The *Saturday Visiter* contest brought Poe in contact with its judges. He corresponded with Miller. Latrobe spoke with him afterwards and enjoyed listening to him express his literary ambitions. Poe had many ideas for stories which he enthusiastically shared. Latrobe recalled that as Poe spoke "he seemed to forget the world around him, as wild fancy, logical truth, mathematical analysis, and wonderful combinations of fact flowed, in strange commingling, from his lips, in words choice and appropriate as though the result of the closest study."[47] After Philadelphia publishers Carey, Lea, and Blanchard brought out a new edition of John Herschel's *Treatise on Astronomy* in February 1834, Poe imagined a story describing life on the moon.[48] Latrobe remembered, "He related to me all the facts of a voyage to the moon, I think, which he proposed to put upon paper, with an accuracy of minute detail and a truthfulness as regarded philosophical phenomena, which impressed you with the idea, almost, that he had himself just returned from the journey which existed only in his imagination."[49] In other words, Poe orally rehearsed what would become "Hans Phaall," the story which marks the beginnings of modern science fiction.

Poe also shared his idea for "Hans Phaall" with John P. Kennedy. Overall, Kennedy was more important to Poe than Latrobe, for he had more contacts among publishers and editors. With the publication of *Swallow Barn*, Kennedy had firmly established his reputation in the world of letters, so he was in an excellent position to help Poe. He encouraged him to publish his "Tales of the Folio Club" as a book. With such encouragement, Poe entrusted the manuscript to Kennedy who sent it to Carey, Lea, and Blanchard, the firm which had published *Swallow Barn*. Kennedy also managed to find some odd jobs for Poe to help sustain him during his lean years in Baltimore. The death of John Allan in March 1834, an event Poe had expected would lift him from his poverty, had no such effect, for Allan left him nothing. The situation made Poe all the more anxious to publish his volume of tales, so he urged Kennedy to have Carey, Lea, and Blanchard expedite publication of the "Folio Club" volume, for the firm had held onto it for what seemed an unreasonable length of time. With Lambert Wilmer, Poe looked forward to the day

> When bards no more with trembling hope shall wait
> While Carey's clerks examine and debate,
> And all the dreams of recompense dispel,
> When verse is found too sensible to sell![50]

Henry C. Carey eventually let Kennedy know that he was willing to publish the tales as a separate volume, but that he did not expect to profit from it: "Such little things rarely succeed, and if they do, their produce is small. I do not expect to make anything, but am perfectly willing to take the chance of it."[51] Recognizing the book's unlikely prospects, Carey was unwilling to pay its author in advance. Instead, he suggested that a surer and more expedient way for Poe to make money from his tales would be to offer one to Eliza Leslie for her annual, *The Gift: A Christmas and New Year's Present*, a work Poe would later characterize as "highly creditable to the enterprise of its publishers, and more so to the taste and talents of Miss Leslie."[52] Overall, Carey suggested, piecemeal publication of the stories in the annuals would generate more income than the publication of a single volume. He let Kennedy know that he was more than willing to do what he could to help his friend's literary career, yet Carey's ultimate conclusion was disappointing: "I should be exceedingly glad to promote your friend's objects if I knew how, but writing is a very poor business unless a man can find the way of taking the public attention, and *that is not often done by short stories*. People want something larger and longer."[53] Without consulting Poe, Kennedy told Carey to let Eliza Leslie see the manuscript volume and choose a tale for *The Gift*, providing the same tale could be republished as part of Poe's volume of tales. Leslie chose "MS. in a Bottle" and paid one dollar per page making a total of fifteen dollars.[54]

Kennedy also helped bring Poe in contact with Richmond editor Thomas W. White. After White had first proposed the *Southern Literary Messenger* in 1834, Kennedy applauded his efforts and hinted that he would be willing to contribute to the new monthly magazine. Encouraged by Kennedy and many others, White launched the *Southern Literary Messenger*, the most ambitious literary journal the South had seen. The first issue appeared in August 1834. Early the next year, Kennedy instructed Poe to contribute to the *Southern*

Literary Messenger and wrote to White, asking him to take Poe on in an editorial capacity.[55] White subsequently accepted "Berenice" for the March 1835 issue and "Morella" for the April issue. In addition, White agreed to have Poe write the critical notices for the April issue.

Poe was grateful for the opportunity White offered him and did his best to promote the *Southern Literary Messenger* in Baltimore. He reviewed the April, May, and June issues of the *Messenger* for the Baltimore press. Though he was willing to promote the magazine, his reviews show that he was unwilling to compromise his literary standards. Poe's reviews in the *Baltimore Republican and Commercial Advertiser* and the *Baltimore American* demonstrate that he appreciated White's efforts but that he was not afraid to critique what needed to be critiqued. Reviewing an essay on contemporary American fiction in the May 1835 issue, for example, Poe noted the author's neglect of Robert Montgomery Bird and John Pendleton Kennedy and remarked, "The Article on *Recent American Novels* is crude and undigested. – The writer is evidently unacquainted with his theme."[56] Reviewing the June 1835 *Messenger*, the issue containing "Hans Phaall," Poe stated, "We do not . . . like the *Old Parish Church, by Nugator*. The hop, skip, and jump metre, whose grotesque air is heightened by means of double rhymes, is, to say the least, little in accordance with the solemnity of the subject. Some of the words are even misspelt, and not a few of the allusions are exceedingly low."[57] The acumen Poe demonstrates in these early reviews shows that his critical abilities were already well developed and indicates his nascent editorial ability.

Poe contributed stories, poems, and reviews to the *Southern Literary Messenger* that spring and summer. After his reviews helped significantly boost the magazine's circulation, White agreed to hire him as editorial assistant and principal book reviewer. To fulfill the responsibility, Poe would have to forsake Baltimore for Richmond, but that was a small price to pay. He would have to leave Virginia Clemm and her mother, but they would eventually join him in Richmond. Besides, Poe had fond memories of Richmond and, with John Allan dead, the town no longer held any animosity for him. Baltimore may have had a lively book culture in the early 1830s, but the city offered little opportunity for anyone who longed to be a literary professional.

CHAPTER 4

Booksellers' banquet

This was the greatest dinner I was ever at . . .
                                                    – Philip Hone

Edgar Allan Poe's association with the *Southern Literary Messenger* gave
him an opportunity unprecedented in his personal experience. It
brought him greater intimacy with the printed word than he had yet
known, permitted him the chance to read a nearly countless number
of publications, and allowed him an extraordinary opportunity to
broaden his base of knowledge and deepen his understanding of
contemporary print culture. Books from the prominent New York
and Philadelphia publishers, virtually every newspaper from Virginia
and all the major papers from Boston to Savannah, every important
magazine in America, and the British quarterlies passed across his
desk at the *Southern Literary Messenger* office. While there, he wrote
nearly all of the reviews for the magazine. Taking advantage of the
editorial freedom White allowed him, Poe ably developed his unique
critical voice. The *Messenger* provided a vehicle for his imaginative
literature as well, White paying extra for any stories or verse
published in the magazine. In large part, Poe's critical notices
generated more notoriety for him than his creative work, though
some of his finest early tales and verse appeared in the magazine.

Poe left the *Southern Literary Messenger* for several reasons. For one,
White refused to pay the salary Poe demanded. He and Virginia had
married in 1836, and Poe had found the wages of an editorial
assistant – ten dollars a week – inadequate to support his household.
Furthermore, White had begun quibbling with the editorial free-
doms Poe was taking. Poe, more than once too often, had also let his
bête noire – his intolerance to alcohol – get the better of him. After
leaving the *Southern Literary Messenger* in January 1837, Edgar and
Virginia Poe, along with her mother, Maria Clemm, moved to New

York where Mrs. Clemm took in boarders to support the family while Eddie, as she called her son-in-law, looked for work as an editor. Poe had no definite prospects for employment, though he had written to New York before leaving Richmond. The success of the *Southern Literary Messenger* during his tenure with the magazine gave him confidence that a New York magazine would welcome his editorial services.

Mrs. Clemm's boarders included the rare-book dealer William Gowans who became good friends with Poe. Gowans later recalled, "For eight months, or more, 'one house contained us, us one table fed.' During that time I saw much of him, and had an opportunity of conversing with him often . . . he was one of the most courteous, gentlemanly, and intelligent companions I have met."[1] Gowans had entered the book business ten years before as a clerk, but he soon had a bookstall of his own, which became profitable enough to allow him to open a store. Gowans's reputation as a rare-book dealer had been growing with every year, and his clientele included some of the city's most well-known bookmen. Gowans had begun making some tentative efforts as a publisher, issuing an edition of Plato and reprinting a literary miscellany. Gowans would later distinguish his list of publications with the "Bibliotheca Americana" series, which included new editions of two rare works important to the history of colonial promotion literature: George Alsop's *A Character of the Province of Maryland* and Daniel Denton's *Brief Description of New York*, a work Poe found to be "of exceeding interest – to say nothing of its value in an historical point of view."[2] Poe may have exercised a lasting influence on Gowans's list. In the *Southern Literary Messenger*, Poe had called for an American edition of Coleridge's *Biographia Literaria*. Wiley and Putnam issued an American edition in 1847 but afterwards let it go out of print. Gowans bought the Wiley and Putnam plates and republished the work in 1852.[3] In Gowans, Poe found a kindred spirit, and, much like the Baltimore bookshops, Gowans's store provided a place for Poe to dawdle and read. There, Gowans may have shown his friend many rare books he could hardly have encountered elsewhere.[4]

Gowans also put Poe in contact with publishers, editors, and others in New York's world of books. He was likely responsible for bringing Poe to the Booksellers' Dinner. The general purpose of the banquet was to encourage the book business by promoting good feelings among the various members of the contemporary print culture: authors, booksellers, editors, illustrators, and publishers. The *Morning Courier and New-York Enquirer,* finding the event a great success, hoped it would foster similar gatherings regularly "to draw the lonely and meditative scholar from his books, and place him, at least from time to time, in communion with his fellows – the great body of those whose kindred to him in occupation, assures him of sympathy always[,] often of instruction . . . the almost helpless Man of Books and that work day world beyond his cloister, of which he knows so little, and with which he is usually so unfit to deal."[5]

The banquet was sponsored by the booksellers of New York City, which is to say that it was sponsored by the booksellers and publishers. In Poe's time, there was no clear dividing line between the two. Many publishers had their own retail stores, and booksellers, like Gowans, often made publishing ventures. The Committee of Arrangements included several of the day's most prominent publishers: George Dearborn, the man responsible for publishing the poetry of Joseph Rodman Drake and Fitz-Greene Halleck and who, as Poe saw it, was largely responsible for creating their undeserved reputation;[6] George P. Putnam, who would soon form a partnership with John Wiley which would become one of the most influential publishing firms during the next decade and which would publish Poe's 1845 *Tales* as well as *The Raven and Other Poems* as part of their important series, "Wiley and Putnam's Library of American Books"; and Fletcher Harper, one of the heads of Harper and Brothers, New York City's largest and most powerful publisher and – with the possible exception of Carey, Lea, and Blanchard in Philadelphia – the largest publisher in the United States. James, another of the Harper brothers, also attended the banquet. David Felt, a lesser publisher and bookseller who specialized in short, popular, low-risk works such as almanacs and chapbooks, presided. John Keese, a bookseller who would soon become both editor and anthologizer, served as toastmaster. After Keese's anthology, *The Poets of America,* appeared two years later, Poe recognized his fine taste, sound judgment, and knowledge of American poetry. The two later corresponded.[7]

At five o'clock in the evening on 30 March, 1837, the leading literary figures of the day began gathering at the City Hotel in Lower Broadway.[8] Erected in 1794, the City Hotel was the first building in the United States designed specifically for use as a hotel, and it had established a reputation for the prestigious social functions held in its large assembly hall. All in all, it was the finest hotel in New York and, according to one observer, "without an equal in the United States."[9] (It would be destroyed in 1849 to make way for more lucrative commercial properties.) The assembly hall was decorated for the occasion, its niches filled with fine busts of Benjamin Franklin, Washington Irving, John Milton, Sir Walter Scott, and William Shakespeare. Portraits of other authors and some statesmen adorned the walls. Never had the City Hotel – or any other hotel – contained as many prominent figures in American literature. As the *Evening Post* commented, "The Dinner was served in the best *taste*, and was partaken of by many whose names are familiar as household words, to the reading world. It was truly a brilliant assembly, and such an one as rarely occurs."[10] Philip Hone, quondam mayor of New York whose lasting reputation rests on the detailed diary he kept during the early nineteenth century, returned to the City Hotel the next morning to talk over the event with the hotel's proprietor from whom he learned that 277 people – that is – men sat down to dinner.[11] Though the contemporary publishers welcomed the efforts of women writers, they did not welcome them to such social gatherings as the Booksellers' Dinner. (Remember, this was the same year the Grimké sisters made such a stir by speaking to a combined male and female audience.) In Poe's day, it was more acceptable for women to appear in print than it was for them to appear in public. A similar gathering sponsored by the booksellers two decades later welcomed female authors, yet this later festival differed significantly, for it was held during the day as a luncheon, and no alcohol was served.[12]

While Poe's stint with the *Southern Literary Messenger* had established his reputation as a tough-minded book reviewer and, to a lesser extent, as an author of weird tales, he had yet to make any significant contacts among New York's literati. The dinner gave Poe the chance to speak with the editors or proprietors of magazines who might be willing to give him a job and publishers who might be interested in publishing his work. The second periodical installment of "Pym" had appeared in the *Southern Literary Messenger* earlier that month, and the book-length version was finished – or nearly so. Any publisher who had read the two periodical installments would need little convincing to publish the complete book.

Though Poe was familiar with the work of nearly every author and editor in attendance, he had met few of them. They, in turn, were familiar with his editorial work from reading the critical notices in the *Southern Literary Messenger*, which, as Poe later admitted in retrospect, reflected a "somewhat overdone causticity."[13] Some of the banqueteers appreciated Poe's hardnosed reviews and had said so in print. Among the newspapermen in attendance, Colonel James Watson Webb, editor of the *Morning Courier*, had applauded Poe's critical notices, calling them the "boldest, the most independent, and unflinching, of all that appears in the periodical world." Mordecai Noah, who would befriend Poe and later testify to his character in his libel suit against Thomas Dunn English, also had applauded the *Southern Literary Messenger* and found Poe's critical notices "written with uncommon spirit" and "judiciously directed against the mawkish style and matter of those ephemeral productions with which, under the name of *chef-d'oeuvres* in novel writing, the poor humbugged public are so unmercifully gagged and bamboozled."[14]

Other important newspaper and magazine editors came to the Booksellers' Dinner: Lewis Gaylord Clark, the editor who would take Poe to task in the pages of the *Knickerbocker*; Richard Adams Locke, the author of the famous "Moon Hoax" who was now working as an editor; Charles King, editor of the *New York American*; and George P. Morris, founder-editor of the *New-York Mirror*. General Morris, as he was known, was also a songwriter and poet, the roles in which Poe most appreciated him. Poe wrote, "Morris is, very decidedly, our best writer of songs – and, in saying this, I mean to assign him a high rank as *poet*."[15] Morris shared the editing of the *New-York Mirror* with Theodore S. Fay and the young dandy, Nathaniel P. Willis. Morris and Willis later would collaborate again to form the *Home Journal*. (As Poe wrote, together they were known as "mi-boy and the Brigadier.") Willis was also invited to the Booksellers' Dinner, but, unable to attend, he sent his regrets.

The only major journalist not invited was James Gordon Bennett, editor and proprietor of the New York *Herald*. Bennett, too, had a reputation for his causticity, and his frequently disdainful critiques had offended many within New York's world of books. In "The Literary Life of Thingum Bob," Poe would list Bennett among several other harsh critics.[16] After the banquet, Bennett placed many brief reports in the *Herald* deriding the event and its booksellers for deliberately neglecting him. One report suggested that the "committee of invitations, after a long debate, accomplished the glorious victory of rejecting a proposition to invite James Gordon Bennett, who passes himself off for an editor, wit, author, philosopher, poet, historian, metaphysician, entirely on his own hook, without any aid or assistance from literary puffery or intrigue. It is very doubtful, we learn, whether Bennett would have attended any dinner, for he generally prefers a solitary chicken and a bottle of London porter, to the best turn out in town."[17] By this account, Bennett would have us believe that he missed the event, but make no mistake, invitation or not, he showed up, stayed until late, and, in fact, got so caught up in the proceedings that he volunteered a toast to the "American Newspaper Press – Stars of the first magnitude, fit to adorn a constellation in any hemisphere."[18]

Not all of the newspapermen would have welcomed Poe with open arms. William L. Stone, editor of the *Commercial Advertiser,* would have resented the young whippersnapper's presence. Less than a year before, Poe had "used up" Colonel Stone's anonymously published *Ups and Downs in the Life of a Distressed Gentleman*, concluding his critical notice: "We have given the entire pith and marrow of the book. The term *flat*, is the only general expression which would apply to it. It is written, we believe, by Col. Stone of the New York Commercial Advertiser, and should have been printed among the quack advertisements in a spare corner of his paper."[19] In the pages of his own paper, Stone had parried Poe's attacks and asserted that the majority of the critical notices in the *Southern Literary Messenger* were "flippant, unjust, untenable and uncritical."[20]

America's most prominent and well-known poet, Fitz-Greene Halleck, also attended the Booksellers' Dinner. He, too, scarcely would have welcomed Poe. The previous year, Poe had reviewed Halleck's *Alnwick Castle, with Other Poems* along with the posthumous collection of verse by Joseph Rodman Drake, *The Culprit Fay, and Other Poems*. Though Poe did not condemn Halleck as brusquely as he had Stone, his negative review is notable, for Halleck had met near universal approval at the hands of other contemporary critics. Poe found Halleck's poetical abilities less than those of his dead friend Drake, however, and the best praise Poe could muster was to say that Halleck's writing evidenced a certain *"sportive elegance."*[21] Though it may have seemed harsh then, Poe's criticism was on target. Nowadays, both Drake and Halleck go unread and are remembered only as the subjects of Poe's Drake–Halleck review. Poe may or may not have spoken with Halleck on this occasion, but he later expressed a familiarity with the poet's personal mannerisms: "He converses fluently, with animation and zeal; is choice and accurate in his language, exceedingly quick at repartee and apt at anecdote."[22]

Another well-known American poet, William Cullen Bryant, joined the festivities. He, too, had recently been reviewed by Poe. Just two months before, Poe had written a lengthy critical notice of the fourth edition of Bryant's *Poems*. Poe thought much more highly of Bryant than of Halleck. Though unwilling to place Bryant among the first rank of modern poets – Shelley, Coleridge, Wordsworth, Keats – Poe did find much to admire in Bryant's verse. His "air of calm and elevated contemplation" made reading his verse a pleasant activity. Though disliking the didacticism of Bryant's work, Poe nevertheless found his poetry worth reading and came to the conclusion: "As a versifier, we know of no writer, living or dead, who can be said greatly to surpass him."[23]

A variety of other authors and men of letters attended the Booksellers's Dinner. The event attracted Alexander Flash, a publisher from Cincinnati, which was fast becoming the publishing center of the West. There, Flash had published a variety of *belles lettres* including Frederick W. Thomas's poem, *The Emigrant, Or, Reflections While Descending the Ohio*, a "rambling poem," as Thomas later described it to Poe.[24] The year before, Poe had reviewed another product of Flash's press, finding that the book supplied "bright hopes for the Literature of the West."[25] Travel writers attending the banquet included the Reverend Orville Dewey. Poe had reviewed *The Old World and the New*, and, though he had critiqued Dewey's *naiveté*, he appreciated the value of juxtaposing the Old and New Worlds. Charles Fenno Hoffman, editor of the *American Monthly Magazine*, had recently published *A Winter in the West*, a travel narrative Poe had called "a work of great sprightliness . . . replete with instruction and amusement."[26] Also attending were New York City's eminent professors. Several from Columbia were there including Charles Anthon, Professor of Greek and Latin, whom Poe recognized as "the most erudite of our classical scholars."[27] Professor George Bush from the newly formed New York University also attended, too. The prolific miscellaneous writers, James Kirke Paulding and Henry William Herbert, whose *The Brothers, A Tale of the Fronde* Poe had appreciated in the *Messenger*, also came.[28]

The most famous author there, however, was Washington Irving.

He was the only guest whose likeness appeared among the busts which adorned the niches of the City Hotel's assembly hall. Irving was no stranger to great dinners. After Philip Hone had called the Booksellers' Dinner the greatest he had ever attended, he qualified himself, adding, "with the exception, perhaps, of that given to Washington Irving on his return from Europe."[29] Poe had yet to meet Irving, but he was acutely aware of Irving's enormous contemporary reputation. Reviewing Irving's *A Tour on the Prairies* not long before, Poe had known enough to pay Irving proper respect: "A book from the pen of Washington Irving, is a *morceau*, which will always be eagerly sought after by literary epicures. He is decidedly one of the most popular writers in this country: his sketches of character and scenery, are always true to the life, full of freshness and vigor; and there is usually a clear stream of thought pervading his pages, in fine contrast with the crude and indistinct conceptions of ordinary writers." Still, Poe was bold enough not to give Irving his unqualified approval and critiqued the monotonous detail contained within *A Tour on the Prairies* as well as the tedium of its setting.[30]

There's no telling how many of these literary notables Poe met this evening. He had read the writings of many, if not most of them, yet he had met few, if any. Not averse to violating social protocol and introducing himself to others, he would have preferred being properly introduced if possible. His friend William Gowans would have helped greatly. Several of the banqueteers were customers of his, and others were business associates. Gowans was on intimate terms with James Harper, so he may have introduced him to Poe.[31] Many of the authors in attendance Poe had corresponded with on behalf of the *Southern Literary Messenger*; such prior contact facilitated personal introductions.

Once the guests had settled at their places for dinner, the Revd. J. F. Schroeder said grace and, in so doing, reminded the "great assembly of the writers and publishers of books, of the great Book of Books and the Author of Authors."[32] Schroeder's remarks set the tone for the evening, and metaphoric uses of the word "book" and the idea of authorship recurred with numbing frequency from the first speech through to the last toast. After Schroeder's invocation, the guests sat down to "one of the best conducted and plenteous feasts" that New York had ever seen.[33]

After dinner, John Keese fulfilled his role as toastmaster. A fine public speaker, Keese would make a reputation as a book-auctioneer and, indeed, would earn for himself the title, "prince of auctioneers." Evert Duyckinck remembered that "few who attended his sales did not carry away with them some recollection of his sparkling genius." For nearly every book put on the block, Keese knew something about its subject or its author which provided "some opportunity for his pleasantry." He never failed to "eke out his merriment with some innocent play upon his audience."[34] On this occasion, according to James Gordon Bennett, Keese "made a splendid speech."[35] He alluded to Sydney Smith's memorable query, "Who reads an American book?": "The unworthy sarcasm which was once levelled at our national literature has long since sought the oblivion of those who uttered it, and the emanations of American talent, bearing the imprint of American publishers, have assumed a proud eminence beside the literature of the old world." Keese next made the predictable analogy between American liberty and American literature. He then emphasized that American publishers and booksellers should do whatever they could to foster and reward native literary talent. Speaking for all the publishers and booksellers present, Keese said, "[W]e deem it to be our *interest* liberally to extend to American authors those solid and substantial advantages, for the want of which, in a previous age, so many of the literary men of Europe died in penury and neglect; men, of whose intellectual labors the booksellers will long continue to reap the rich reward." Poe had yet to reap such rewards, but, to be sure, Keese's words sounded hopeful.

Taking into account the vastness of America and the near universal literacy of its people, Keese emphasized the advantage the United States, "from the white hills of New England to the orange groves of Florida," had "for the circulation and consumption of *intellectual produce*." Closing his speech, Keese began the regular or planned toasts. Besides these, there were literally dozens of impromptu, volunteer toasts. The regular toasts were interspersed with speeches, additional toasts, and songs sung by the tenor John Jones, and the swarthy-visaged bass Henry Russell, with orchestral accompaniment. The songs were received with "loud acclamations of applause." There is no need to recount many of the toasts – though the day's fullest newspaper accounts did – yet several are worth repeating, for few recorded expressions better capture the mood of literary America around the mid-1830s. The third regular toast, for example, honored "American Authors and Authors the

World over – Benefactors of the human race, and especially deserving *our* gratitude as furnishing the means whereby we live." Afterwards, Jones and Russell sang a rousing chorus of "We are all good fellows together."

The fifth regular toast was to the "Editors of the Periodical Press – Guardians of our Literature, and Sentinels upon the watch-tower of our Liberties, they wield a power which may dethrone a monarch or elevate a people." After the toast, Colonel Stone had much to say regarding the state of publishing in America. Far less entertaining a speaker than John Keese, Stone loaded his remarks with ponderous statistics emphasizing the size and value of American book production. His most provocative comments concerned the kinds of books issued by American publishers compared to those works reprinted from abroad. According to Stone's numbers, speculative and useful works dominated American book production while the best imaginative works came from abroad. Accompanying Stone's remarks, Jones and Russell sang "Clare de Kitchen." Poe's thoughts are unrecorded, but his kindred spirit, James Gordon Bennett, found the tune especially appropriate:

It is a remarkable commentary on the fine taste – the exquisite taste – the refined taste – the pure taste – the classic taste of the committee of *savans* who concocted it, and the body of editors who drank it. 'Clare de Kitchen!' Bravo! What beauty and propriety in the selection! What exquisite sensibility in the strain!

The editors of New York, with the booksellers, all cooked up in the same pot, would furnish a genuine dish to posterity.[36]

The seventh regular toast, which was followed by "Auld Lang Syne," acclaimed "Books – the best of friends, for they never change, never obtrude, and never ask favors that it is difficult to grant." The ninth regular toast honored "The Booksellers of Boston – Their notions about books, and trade, and good dinners, amazingly cute and clever." Jones and Russell sang "Yankee Doodle" after the toast. (Later, Poe would have the lunatic band in "The System of Doctor Tarr and Professor Fether" play "Yankee Doodle.") Representing the Boston booksellers, Harrison Gray arose to speak. True to Boston's Puritan legacy, Gray beheld the "glittering display of beakers filled with libations to the jolly god" and suggested, "It was a maxim of the Pilgrims, that it was not good for a man to drink anything stronger than water. In drinking to the sentiment which I am about to propose, I would respectfully ask you

. . . to do it in the element with which Adam pledged Eve." Gray's suggestion was met with a fair amount of grumbling, but, undaunted, he raised his tumbler of Adam's ale and toasted, "Schools and Colleges – Let us cherish and support them. They mould the minds that make the merchandise we trade in, and are ever creating a market for us."

The eleventh regular toast: "Printing – The only black art whose exercise raises man to a superior order of intelligence, and whose magic creates and destroys fairy palaces of thought." After the toast, Jones and Russell sang the incantation scene from Carl Maria von Weber's *Der Freischutz* and Charles King spoke. Unlike so many of the other speakers, King refrained from jingoism. Instead, he spoke of the common bond which all intellectual souls shared regardless of nationality, the "interests and aims of the highest dignity, which united to the various branches of knowledge, literature and art. They were all citizens of one great republic, allegiance to which were both grateful and easy – the Republic of Letters; where the only strife was, who should do the most and go the fartherest for the interests and honor of all."

Others reiterated the idea. At one point, the comments made by those who sent their regrets were read. Conveying his regrets, Nathaniel P. Willis honored the Republic of Letters. Mordecai Noah, who was called to speak after the regular toasts were over, gave a speech "full of eloquence and Bonhomme." Ending his remarks, Noah toasted, "The Republic of Letters – Which has for its subjects the learned of every clime, and the genius of every country." Poe appreciated the idea which King, Willis, and Noah expressed and later would use it himself to promote his periodical venture. In a prospectus for his literary periodical, Poe asserted that the magazine would "support the general interests of the Republic of Letters, and insist upon regarding the world at large as the sole proper audience for their author."[37]

Soon, Washington Irving was asked to speak. His remarks also were designed to promote good feelings between both sides of the Atlantic. Irving wished to toast to the health of his friend, the British poet Samuel Rogers, characterizing him as "an enlightened and liberal friend of America and Americans" whose "great influence in the world of literature and the fine arts" allowed him to bring youthful American artists and writers to the attention of the British public. He then read an extract from a recent letter he had received from Rogers which extravagantly praised the poems of Fitz-Greene Halleck, asserting that they were "better than any thing we can do just now on our side [of] the Atlantic," an assertion prompting a loud cheer from those in attendance. It is sometimes difficult to distinguish individual voices amidst a clamor, yet one cannot help but imagine that Poe's cheer sounded more like a guffaw. Irving concluded with a toast to "*Samuel Rogers* – The friend of American genius."[38] The banqueteers rose and drank the toast standing.

After the series of speeches, it became time for the volunteer toasts. The publishers, booksellers, and the newspaper press were toasted multiple times. Fletcher Harper, for example, toasted the magnanimity of booksellers: "Generous individuals, who kindly assist Authors to obtain an immortality in which they do not themselves participate." As the toasts continued with no end in sight, Chairman David Felt retired for the evening and let Fletcher Harper take over as chair. Fletcher's brother James proposed a toast to "The memory of Walter Scott, and other illustrious authors, who, in our own time, have built up intellectual temples for the admiration of future ages, and rested from their labors." The guests stood for the toast. George Dearborn toasted the memory of Faust. Though it may seem unusual to toast a legendary necromancer, Dearborn was following the popular association between Dr. Faustus and Johann Fust, the early German printer and contemporary of Gutenberg. Poe had little respect for Dearborn and would have recognized his vulgar error. Over a year before, Poe had reviewed William Godwin's *Lives of the Necromancers* and observed, "The prevalent idea that Fust, the printer, and Faustus the magician, were identical, is here very properly contradicted."[39]

After countless other toasts, Poe provided one of his own: "The Monthlies of Gotham – Their distinguished Editors, and their vigorous Collaborateurs." Since Poe hoped to find employment with one of the monthlies of Gotham, his remarks are unabashedly self-serving. Still, they remain good-hearted. Other volunteer toasts kept the festivities going until the small hours. Overall, the affair was a brilliant success.

Imagine Poe's journey home from the City Hotel. He probably walked. The omnibuses had stopped running and hiring a coach was beyond his means. Besides, it was only a half-dozen or so blocks, nothing for a good athlete like Poe. The walk would give him time to think. The city had begun to install gas lamps, yet they were spaced so far apart that the streets were more dark than light. Beyond earshot of the boisterous throng leaving the City Hotel late that evening, the streets were quiet. Poe could not help but feel good about his decision to come to New York. How faraway and insignificant his former haunts now appeared. The banqueteers had toasted the booksellers and publishers of Boston and Philadelphia, and the occasion had even attracted one publisher from Cincinnati, yet no one toasted the booksellers and publishers of Richmond or Baltimore. Within America's dominant literary community, the South scarcely seemed to matter. Poe had likely talked to the Harpers and therefore brought *The Narrative of Arthur Gordon Pym* one step closer to publication in book form. He had no definite prospects for employment, yet he could not help but feel hopeful. He had not personally offended anyone. At least the contemporary accounts do not mention anyone disturbing the general conviviality. The *Evening Post*, for example, said that uncommon "animation and enthusiasm" combined with "good order and excellent feeling" prevailed throughout the evening. Poe's apparent restraint is especially notable considering Charles King's toast to Richard Adams Locke as "The Author of the modern Discoveries in the Moon." The fact that he was able to articulate himself late in the evening after numerous toasts suggests that he had managed to keep his *bête noire* in abeyance. Perhaps he took Harrison Gray's advice and stuck to Adam's ale, but perhaps he was simply one of the many dinner guests "abundantly inspirited by the feast of reason."[40] For one night, his literary ambitions seemed to be coming true.

CHAPTER 5

The novel

Readers in this country have a decided and strong preference
for works (especially fiction) in which a single and connected
story occupies the whole volume, or number of volumes, as the
case may be.

– Harper and Brothers to Poe, June 1836

Discouraged from publishing his "Tales of the Folio Club" with
Philadelphia's largest publisher, Edgar Allan Poe turned to New
York's. The year before Poe came to Gotham, he corresponded with
one of its foremost literary figures as well as its leading publisher. Just
as he had sought John Pendleton Kennedy's assistance to place the
collection of tales with Carey, Lea, and Blanchard, Poe sought James
Kirke Paulding's help to place the book with the Harpers. Paulding
had established his literary reputation three decades before with
Salmagundi, an essay collection he wrote with Washington Irving, and
continued it through his satirical yet good-hearted *Letters from the
South* and such historical novels as *Koningsmarke; or, Old Times in the
New World*. Starting in 1834, the Harpers began issuing a collected
edition of Paulding's writings, a projected twelve- or fifteen-volume
set. Poe did not know Paulding personally, but his employer, Thomas
W. White, had corresponded with him. Poe contacted him through
White and convinced him to take possession of his manuscript and
to bring it to the Harpers' attention. Paulding was aware of the
critical notices in the *Southern Literary Messenger* and admired Poe's
literary abilities; he did not mind doing a favor for the younger man.
Paulding had less influence over the Harpers than White and Poe
had assumed, however, and he could not convince the firm to
undertake the "Tales of the Folio Club."[1]

The Harpers declined the work for several reasons. Since the tales
had been published separately in the magazines already, they lacked

novelty. Also, Poe's stories were often too obscure to suit the general reader, as the Harpers told Paulding and reiterated in a separate letter to Poe. Furthermore, a longer, book-length narrative was more suitable for publication than a collection of short stories. Though Poe sought to give the volume-length work unity by creating a narrative framework and bridging the separate tales with burlesque criticism, it still could not pass muster as a single narrative. Republished magazine articles, the Harpers told Poe bluntly, "are the most unsaleable of all literary performances."[2] In other words, the firm rejected the "Tales of the Folio Club" using the same basic reason Henry Carey had used to dissuade Poe from publishing the work with his firm. After the Harpers' rejection, Poe continued to seek a publisher for the work, yet he also took their advice to heart and decided to write a book-length narrative.

Of course, the decision did not happen all at once, nor was it made without reservation. Poe's editorial experience at the *Southern Literary Messenger* had given him ample opportunity to develop his critical precepts, and he felt much uncertainty toward the novel and its various subgenres. The historical novel, which Sir Walter Scott had raised to a new level of artistry, was immensely popular, but it held little interest for Poe. Gothic novels had their heyday earlier in the century, yet continued to be written, published, and sold. Specific settings created other fictional subgenres. Sea novels, for example, were becoming increasingly popular among both British and American readers. Another type of book-length fictional narrative, the imaginary voyage, though categorized as a novel nowadays, was infrequently seen as such in Poe's time. Nor was the term "imaginary voyage" used. The reading public considered imaginary voyages with real voyages and travels. For centuries, even the most truthful travellers' tales were not without hyperbole, and the reader of non-fiction voyages generally accepted brief forays into the fantastic with a nod and a chuckle. When travel writers exceeded the limits of the acceptable fantastic, readers took offense – unless, of course, they recognized the work as an intentional fiction created for a didactic purpose.

As imaginary voyages had developed since the days of Sir Thomas More's *Utopia* three centuries before, they had changed little, for they continued to satirize contemporary society and to provide a utopian alternative to it. In other words, they perpetuated the long-standing notion that literature must both delight and instruct. For his short stories, Poe had repudiated the idea in favor of a forward-thinking attitude toward literature as solely an aesthetic object, something which delights yet need not instruct. Being a relatively new literary genre, the short story had yet to receive much critical scrutiny, so it escaped the standards by which book-length narratives were judged. Books, because of their length as well as their publication as distinct works, were bound by stricter rules than short stories. Most novels in Poe's day contained characters who exemplified proper moral conduct, and imaginary voyages often taught by satirizing the faults and foibles of contemporary society. Poe, on the other hand, foresaw a work with no particular instructive purpose. Though the *dénouement* of the book-length narrative he would write is seen today as an object lesson on the dangers of slavery, none of the contemporary reviewers saw it as such, and it is unlikely Poe intended it to be. Considering the disparity between his own aesthetic notions and those by which contemporary books were judged, Poe faced a dilemma: could he write a book-length narrative without compromising his aesthetic principles?

Not only did the conservative standards by which novels were judged violate Poe's aesthetic, but also the sheer length of a novel made Poe question its ability to achieve a high level of artistry. Poe believed that a literary work should be finely crafted and, following Coleridge, he believed that every word counted. To that end, Poe went one better than Coleridge: not only did every word count, the placement of every word counted. Poe was a meticulous literary craftsman, and he believed that a long story could never achieve the tale's level of craftsmanship. (American literature would wait until Henry James for a writer who brought such meticulous craftsmanship to the novel.) The need to maintain suspense and to keep a story going over hundreds of pages, Poe believed, required the author to supply much additional exposition and incidental detail which did not enhance the story's effectiveness or, to use Poe's critical terminology, contribute to its totality of effect. Reviewing Robert M. Bird's *Hawks of Hawk-Hollow*, Poe thought the author's "subject appears always ready to fly away from him. He dallies with it continually – hovers incessantly round it, and about it – and not until driven to exertion by the necessity of bringing his volumes to a close, does he finally grasp it with any appearance of energy or good will."[3] Short stories allowed authors tight control of plot, action, and character, providing the opportunity to tell a highly compact tale, layering multiple levels of meaning one atop another.

Given his objections to the novel, it is a wonder Poe decided to write a book-length fictional narrative at all, but he was still struggling for literary fame, and he well knew that contemporary novelists were garnering more attention than other imaginative writers. After deciding to write a book-length narrative, Poe also had to decide what kind of book to write. When Paulding let him know that the Harpers had rejected the "Tales of the Folio Club," he advised Poe to "apply his fine humor, and his extensive acquirements, to more familiar subjects of satire; to the faults and foibles of our own people, their peculiarities of habits and manners."[4] In other words, he said, "Write like me, and you will succeed." Though Paulding gave Poe a formula for literary success, he did not tell him that he could make a living with his pen. A prolific writer himself, Paulding was not a professional one. His books had achieved a fair amount of popular acclaim, but by no means did he depend on writing to survive. Rather, he had a completely separate career; he held an upper-level administrative position with the US Navy. Poe appreciated Paulding's writing yet realized that it was largely derivative – Addison and Steele as filtered through Sir Walter Scott. Poe refused to change his writing style or mimic successful authors simply for the sake of creating a marketable product.

The longest story he had written so far, "Hans Phaall," gave Poe a possible idea: he could write another imaginary voyage. Though "Hans Phaall" had been overshadowed by the success of Richard A. Locke's "Moon Hoax," by no means had the hoax genre been exhausted. Rather, Locke's notoriety reinforced the popular potential for outrageous narratives feigning truth. Jealous of the other's success, Poe analyzed the differences between his story and Locke's and came to the conclusion that they differed most significantly in tone. Whereas he had written "Hans Phaall" in a "tone of banter," Locke had written earnestly.[5] Though he would never have admitted it, Poe learned from Locke. In his next imaginary voyage, he would include some far-fetched detail, yet he would forsake banter and assume a serious tone.

The literary hoax had a counterpart in the oral tradition, the tall tale, a folk genre which may have influenced Poe. Though Poe largely avoided using folklore in more obvious ways such as making familiar folk character-types into fictional characters, he appreciated extravagant tales and legends. He may have had little contact with adventurers who recounted their fantastic exploits, but personal legends often appeared in the day's newspapers under the guise of truth. In Poe's day, folk and print culture frequently overlapped; as folk narratives made their way into print, printed works became part of the oral tradition. The names of the most famous outrageous travel writers, for example, became proverbs. Though copies of *Voyages and Adventures* of Fernando Mendes Pinto, the sixteenth-century Spanish travel liar, were hard to come by in nineteenth-century America, his name had become a *blason populaire* used to label any extravagant liar. Poe himself would use it in "A Valentine," a cross-acrostic whose "letters, although naturally lying / Like the knight Pinto – Mendez Ferdinando – / Still form a synonym for Truth."[6] An even more popular label for tall-tale tellers was "Munchausen," after Baron Munchausen, whose fantastic narrative, *Travels and Adventures*, had been translated into English in the late eighteenth century and had gone through countless editions. Since "Hans Phaall" incorporated many traditional motifs – the murderer escaping to the moon in a fantastic craft, for example – and was inspired partially by a tall tale, the traditional Irish story of Daniel O'Rourke who visited the moon on the back of an eagle, Poe conceivably looked to the oral tradition to help inspire his next imaginary voyage.

As he mentally shaped the story, it became a far-fetched imaginary voyage with a serious tone which used tall-tale rhetoric and borrowed traditional motifs. Poe also needed to decide upon a setting. Where could he take his hero? He could not send him to the moon without being accused of plagiarizing Locke or repeating himself, so the sky was off limits, but a land or ocean journey to an unknown place remained possible. In the oral culture, frontiersmen and sailors had the best reputation for tall tales. In the print culture, genuine stories of Western travel proliferated, and narratives of ocean voyages describing great deprivation and suffering had been popular among American readers for decades. In colonial America, *Anson's Voyages* had been the most popular story of ocean travel, and it continued to be widely read in Poe's day. Its mixture of exotic description and dire hardship let readers vicariously circumnavigate the globe. The American West was becoming an increasingly popular setting for romantic fiction; the sea had long been so. Frederick Marryat, the day's most popular sea novelist, greatly appealed to American readers. His tales of ocean adventure were frequently reprinted, and Poe knew several of them. Though Poe found Marryat's writing superficial, he nevertheless felt his influence. After all, he was trying to do something he had never done before, to write a book-length narrative for the popular market.

Among imaginary ocean voyages feigning truth, the most well-known recent example was *Sir Edward Seaward's Narrative of His Shipwreck, and Consequent Discovery of Certain Islands in the Caribbean Sea: with Details of His Residence There, and of Various Extraordinary and Highly Interesting Events in His Life, from the Year 1733 to 1749*, a three-volume work written by Jane Porter yet told as a first-person narrative from her fictional protagonist's point of view. The Harpers had published the work a half-dozen years before, and Poe probably read it in Baltimore during the 1830s. He alluded to *Seaward's Narrative* in his "Tales of the Folio Club," for he named one of the club members "Mr. Solomon Seadrift" and characterized him as a man "who had every appearance of a fish." Much later, Poe expressed his appreciation of the work's verisimilitude.[7]

Seaward's Narrative reminded Poe of *Robinson Crusoe*, a work he had read in his boyhood and had returned to again recently. Just two months before the Harpers rejected the "Tales of the Folio Club" Poe had the opportunity to reread *Robinson Crusoe* in a new edition. The experience let him know that there were some books people could read and enjoy in their adolescence and return to as adults with a deeper, more abiding respect. His review of *Robinson Crusoe* shows that the book started him thinking about the possibilities of writing about an imaginary ocean voyage to a distant and unknown land. Though he asserted that it was no longer possible to write a similar story – "There is positively not a square inch of new ground for any future Selkirk"[8] – one cannot help but see Poe behind these words wondering if someone – himself, perhaps – could indeed write a similar story, a story adolescents as well as adults could appreciate.

At this stage in his writing career, *Robinson Crusoe* represented for Poe the ideal book-length fictional narrative. The work verified that it was possible for a book to achieve popularity among contemporary readers and to continue to be read through the ages. After reviewing the new edition, Poe continued to think about Defoe's book during the next month. Reviewing Lambert Wilmer's *The Confessions of Emilia Harrington*, Poe recalled *Robinson Crusoe* as well as other important writers and works in literary history. In the best fiction,

Poe asserted, the "author utterly loses sight of himself in his theme, and, for the time, identifies his own thoughts and feelings with the thoughts and feelings of fictitious existences. Than the power of accomplishing this perfect identification, there is no surer mark of genius. It is the spell of Defoe. It is the wand of Boccacio. It is the proper enchantment of the Arabian Tales – the gramarye of Scott, and the magic of the Bard of Avon."[9] Heady company for Lambert Wilmer! To be sure, Wilmer was a good friend of Poe's, but he was not *that* good a writer. As he applauded the book Wilmer had written, Poe anticipated the one he himself would write, a narrative he would give over to his fictional narrator–protagonist, one Arthur Gordon Pym.

The first periodical installment of "The Narrative of Arthur Gordon Pym" appeared in the January 1837 issue of the *Southern Literary Messenger*. The second installment came in the February *Messenger*, the publication of which was delayed until early March. By the time the second installment appeared, Poe had left Richmond and made his way to New York. The full narrative may not have been completed, but it must have been almost finished by the time Poe reached New York. At last, Poe had done what the publishers told him to do, written a sustained narrative long enough to fill an entire volume. The Harpers agreed to publish the work, and, in June 1837, they copyrighted it and advertised its forthcoming publication.[10] The speed with which the *Narrative of Arthur Gordon Pym* was accepted and promoted affirmed the enthusiasm expressed at the Booksellers' Dinner two months before. The many speeches given then had encouraged publishers to promote the works of young American authors. The Harpers' willingness to publish *Pym* proved that the banquet eloquence was not empty rhetoric.

Before the Harpers had the opportunity to publish Poe's book, however, an economic event of nationwide significance intervened. Through the first half of the year, businesses failed daily. The country's economic problems became so bad that in May, scarcely six weeks after the Booksellers' Dinner, the New York City banks suspended specie payments, precipitating the "Panic of 1837" and marking one of the worst depressions in American history. The land boom, which had lasted a dozen years, collapsed. Across the country, banks failed and factories closed. The depression was obvious to anyone walking the city streets. Philip Hone recorded: "A deadly calm pervades this lately flourishing city. No goods are selling, no business stirring, no boxes encumber the sidewalks of Pearl street."[11] Every industry was affected – including the publishing industry. The Harpers curtailed their list of new publications, withdrawing works which were not surefire hits and concentrating their efforts on books more certain to make money. Poe's fictional voyage was withheld from publication; John L. Stephens's non-fiction travel narrative, *Incidents of Travel in Egypt, Arabia Petraea, and the Holy Land*, on the other hand, was published. Clearly, the Harpers placed great hope in Stephens.[12] The firm's decision to publish and to promote Stephens's work reminded Poe that non-fictional works remained more respectable and more certain of public approval than fictional ones.

The newspaper accounts of the booksellers' banquet had expressed hope that similar events would occur regularly, but the depression quashed such hopes. Amidst a general industry-wide belt-tightening, authors would wait years for a similar dinner. At the time, Poe simply wanted to put food on the table, yet even that was becoming increasingly difficult. He found no steady employment and little piecemeal work. The only important article he managed to publish in 1837 was a long review of Stephens's *Incidents of Travels*. Since the Harpers had published Stephens's book and not his, Poe would have felt animosity toward Stephens, yet little animosity shows in the review. Poe still depended on the Harpers to publish *Pym*, so he could not critique Stephens harshly and maintain good relations with his would-be publisher. Poe's dependence on the Harpers' continuing favor put him in a difficult spot, for he refused to compromise his critical standards and puff a book which did not deserve puffing. Stephens's book, however, simplified matters, for it was, after all, a very good book, and Poe could say so with honesty. Poe concluded his review: "We take leave of Mr. Stephens with sentiments of hearty respect. We hope it is not the last time we shall hear from him. He is a traveller with whom we shall like to take other journeys . . . Mr. Stephens writes like a man of good sense and sound feeling."[13]

Many other authors were affected by the depression, including James Kirke Paulding, for the Harpers discontinued their multi-volume edition of his collected works. Poe could take heart knowing that he was in good company among the Harpers' authors whose works were withheld from publication, yet the Harpers' decision to stop publication of Paulding's collected works sent the message that a well-established reputation was no guarantee of continued success. Though Paulding himself would have been disappointed with the Harpers' decision, it affected him little personally because he did not depend on his writing as a source of income. The setback had no effect on his career. In fact, Paulding reached the pinnacle of his profession the next year when President Van Buren appointed him Secretary of the Navy.

From the appearance of the Stephens review in October 1837 until the middle of the following year, virtually no evidence survives to document Poe's activities or his whereabouts. By the third week of July, 1838, the Harpers had yet to release the *Narrative of Arthur Gordon Pym*, and Poe had long since exhausted all possibilities for employment in New York City. Disgusted, he left New York for Philadelphia. From there he wrote to Paulding and told him he was ready to abandon the writer's craft and asked him for a clerical position with the US Navy: "Could I obtain the most unimportant Clerkship in your gift – *any thing, by sea or land* – to relieve me from the miserable life of literary drudgery to which I, now, with a breaking heart, submit, and for which neither my temper nor my abilities have fitted me?"[14] The youthful bravado expressed in the *Tamerlane* preface over ten years before – the idea that he was set upon a literary career regardless of the consequences – had disappeared. By mid-1838, Poe had reached his nadir and was ready to abandon the literary life. Before the month ended, the Harpers finally released the *Narrative of Arthur Gordon Pym*.

The book's reception was disappointing. The preface made some readers uneasy, for in it Poe had attempted to reconcile the first half of the book, which had appeared in the *Southern Literary Messenger* under his own name (though told as Pym's first-person narrative) with the second half, supposedly written by Pym. The London *Metropolitan Magazine* commented, "The marvellous story – as we learn from the preface – was first published in an American periodical as a work of fiction. It is a pity it was not left as such. As a romance, some portions of it are sufficiently amusing and exciting; but, when palmed upon the public as a true thing, it cannot appear in any other light than that of a bungling business – an impudent attempt at imposing on the credulity of the ignorant."[15] Those who had read the part which had appeared in the *Messenger* realized the narrative was fiction while those who were unaware of the periodical version were unsure how to take it. Some readers who recognized the narrative as fiction did not recognize the narrator as such. In other words, they assumed a young man named Arthur Gordon Pym had written an outrageous story which he was attempting to pass off as his own true adventures. In a way, Poe had accomplished his task all too well. Characterizing *Robinson Crusoe*, he had said that in the finest books of fiction, the author loses himself and completely identifies with his narrator. Since Poe achieved such identification, the book generally was not recognized as his work, so it did nothing to advance his contemporary reputation. One reader who understood the work's hoax-like quality *and* realized that both the narrative and the narrator were fictional creations assumed that Richard Adams Locke had written it, an assumption which would have irked Poe no end.[16] Among other readers, some were delighted with the author's audacity while others took offense at his deliberate attempt to hoodwink them.

The harshest review came at the hands of William Burton, a comic actor who turned to periodical editing as a sideline and who had issued the first number of *Burton's Gentleman's Magazine* the previous July. Aware of Poe's editorial skill, Burton basically accepted the book's preface and recognized that Poe had had a hand in the *Narrative of Arthur Gordon Pym*, yet he was not positive about Poe's authorship: "Mr. Poe, if not the author of Pym's book, is at least responsible for its publication, for it is stated in the preface that Mr. Poe assured the author that the shrewdness and common sense of the public would give it a chance of being received as truth. We regret to find Mr. Poe's name in connexion with such a mass of ignorance and effrontery." Offended, Burton wrote, "A more impudent attempt at humbugging the public has never been exercised; the voyages of Gulliver were politically satirical, and the adventures of Munchausen, the acknowledged caricature of a celebrated traveller. Sindbad the sailor, Peter Wilkins, and More's Utopia, are confessedly works of imagination; but Arthur Gordon Pym put forth a series of travels outraging possibility, and coolly requires his insulted reader to believe his *ipse dixit*."[17]

Burton's multiple associations help situate the *Narrative of Arthur Gordon Pym* within its literary heritage. "Peter Wilkins" refers to Robert Paltock's *The Life and Adventures of Peter Wilkins*, a work first published in London in 1751 which had gone through many subsequent editions. The New York *Evening Post* also associated *Pym* with *Peter Wilkins*, and the New York *Albion*, the British expatriate paper, linked it with another work Burton mentioned: "[S]uch a tissue of wonderful adventures and escapes we have not read since we perused those of 'Sindbad the Sailor.'"[18] The references suggest that though Burton and others were aware of the literary tradition of imaginary voyages, they were reluctant to admit *Pym* into the tradition. Burton appreciated imaginary voyages as long as they were clearly recognizable as such or as long as they fulfilled a purpose such as humorously caricaturing travel writing, as Burton saw Munchausen doing, or satirizing politics, as *Gulliver's Travels* had done so well. Burton's difficulty with the book fundamentally stemmed from his inability to classify it. Though *Pym* described an imaginary voyage to a fictional place, it did not obviously satirize contemporary society or envision a better alternative. Like the novel, it was set in contemporary times, yet unlike the heroes and heroines of the novel, its characters did not exemplify upright moral behavior. The book seemed to fulfill no didactic function whatsoever.

Whereas Burton associated *Pym* with other imaginary voyages, the British *Monthly Review* specifically associated it with contemporary fiction. In a review essay under the running head, "Novels of the Month," *Pym* was reviewed along with such works as Camilla Needham's *Ada* and Hannah Burdon's *The Lost Evidence*. The *Monthly Review* even apologized for devoting so much space to imaginative – "fanciful and ephemeral" – literature. *Pym* differed from the other novels under review, for it was an "*out and out* romance." The *Monthly Review* found the aesthetic principles the work embodied unsettling. The absence of didacticism was most disturbing. The *Monthly Review* concluded that *Pym*'s "extravagances, and mere attempt, as it would seem, at fancying next to miraculous things, rather than the inculcation of any valuable principles or refinement, put it out of the list of those fictions which are to be recommended as models or for general perusal."[19] The *Monthly Review* understood Poe's aesthetic approach; it was simply unwilling to accept it. The London *Court Gazette* responded similarly. It recognized the book's resemblance to *Robinson Crusoe* – except when it came to its didactic purpose: "The style of the narrative is not an indifferent imitation of that adopted by DeFoe, in his best novel, 'Robinson Crusoe.' In matters of surprise, if not in those which appertain to philosophy and morals, the volume will remind the reader of that popular work."[20]

The *Narrative of Arthur Gordon Pym* received some positive reviews and was reprinted in London – a dozen years later a copy of the cheap London reprint would go round the Rossetti household[21] – yet it did little, if anything, to advance Poe's contemporary reputation. He had given the publishers what they asked for and the public, presumably, what they wanted but to no avail. After the book's disappointing reception, Poe virtually disowned it, an unusual impulse, for he often remained fiercely loyal to the products of his own pen. He continued to revise and recite his earlier and less accomplished works, *Tamerlane* and *Al Aaraaf*, well into the 1840s. In a subsequent letter, Poe admitted to Burton that his criticism of *Pym*, though harsh, was nevertheless valid, and referred to it as a "silly book."[22] In the *Cyclopaedia of American Literature*, Evert Duyckinck commented on the seriousness Poe usually devoted to the products of his pen and found his attitude toward *Pym* strange. Duyckinck wrote that Poe, "who was generally anything but indifferent to the reception of his writings, did not appear in his conversation to pride himself much upon it."[23] *Pym* neither enhanced Poe's literary reputation, nor lifted him from the poverty in which he was mired. The charity of James Pedder and his daughters rescued Poe and his family from the brink of starvation, yet Poe could not rely on charity for survival. He needed steady work. Eventually he appealed to William Burton and offered to help edit *Burton's Gentleman's Magazine*. Either uncertain of Poe's authorship of *Pym* or willing to forgive him for it, Burton respected Poe's editorial skill and agreed to take him on at ten dollars a week, the same money Poe had made and complained about three years earlier with the *Southern Literary Messenger*.

Having secured the regular, though meager, salary, Poe approached the publishing firm of Lea and Blanchard – Henry Carey having retired from the business to pursue a career as a writer on economics – and offered them his short stories. He had abandoned the Folio Club framework but now had a collection large enough to fill a two-volume edition. Poe bolstered his appeal by asserting that he had no urgent need for royalties. The assertion, of course, was a complete lie, but, as Poe saw it, a necessary one to convince the firm to accept the collection. In his letter to Lea and Blanchard, Poe described his work in the most appealing way possible. James Kirke Paulding had earlier advised Poe to write a story sufficient to fill "a couple of volumes, for that is the magical number."[24] Though Poe's work consisted of multiple short stories, he tried to sell it as a connected narrative, for he told them that he had enough text to fill "two novel volumes." In other words, Poe was trying to pass off his collected tales as a novel or something close to it. Poe's willingness to forgo royalties, more than his inference of the collection's novel-like quality, convinced the firm to publish the work in two volumes at their own risk as *Tales of the Grotesque and Arabesque*. It met with a lukewarm response and sold few copies.

Writing for *Burton's Gentleman's Magazine*, Poe was under pressure to fill its columns, yet Burton, unlike Thomas White, did not allow Poe to fill the pages of his magazine with long critical notices. Poe's need to fill magazine space combined with his yet unfulfilled desire for literary fame prompted him to attempt another book-length work, a narrative which could be published serially in *Burton's* and then later assembled in book form. He again decided on an imaginative journey. After fictional adventures to outer space and the Polar Seas, the American West was the only large physical realm yet unexplored by Poe's imagination. The West, however, was becoming increasingly well known to the American reading public. Over three decades had passed since Lewis and Clark ventured west, and countless others had followed them in the interim. In order to describe a journey to unexplored regions, Poe had to set his imaginary voyage a half-century in the past. As a result, the work combined imaginary voyage and historical romance. The result was the *Journal of Julius Rodman*, a work projected in monthly installments which would appear over the course of a year. Poe did not write the entire narrative before he began its serialization. Rather, he wrote it month by month as the installments were needed. His over-reliance on source material and his frequently minimal changes to his source texts show that Poe assembled *Rodman* hastily and that his heart was not in it. Before *Rodman* was half over, Poe and Burton had a falling out. Poe left the magazine and never completed the work.

Poe's desertion of *Rodman* had both a practical and an aesthetic basis. Having written the narrative to fill the pages of *Burton's*, he no longer had to finish it once he left the magazine. Yet there also was an artistic reason why he never came back to *Rodman*, for he found a better way to retell the story of the American West. The work's finest passage, a description of buffalo attempting to cross a river, comes late in the completed portion of *Rodman*. Though borrowed from a source, Poe revised and adapted the passage to make it a microcosm of the American journey to the West. Coming from the East, the buffalo attempt to cross the river, but, unable to ascend its steep western bank, they double-back and return east. Caught in the current they are forced west again and then back east, circling until they perish. The episode is a statement about West-bound adventurers who detach themselves from the East and from civilization, yet are unable to adapt to the wilderness environment of the American West. They become entrapped in a limbo between the past they have left behind and the future they are unable to reach. Ultimately they perish.

The passage is forceful enough to convince readers that Poe might have made something of *Rodman* had he devoted his full attention to it, but Poe found a better way to retell the story of the American journey west. Rodman's narrative was simplistic and over-obvious. Any competent writer could tell a story about the American West set in the American West. Poe, on the other hand, decided to tell a story about the American West set on the coast of Norway. During or after the time he wrote the buffalo scene for *Rodman*, Poe recognized the similarity between the circling buffalo and the famous Norway maelström and realized he could tell a story of the maelström as an analogue for the American West. Early in the story, Poe makes the comparison explicit as he compares the sound of the maelström with that of the buffalo moaning, and the story ends with the setting moon, an analogue for the setting sun. The old Norwegian guide who survives his brothers to narrate the story is a stand-in for the American frontiersman who has survived a wilderness ordeal many others had not survived. Poe not only abandoned *Rodman* because his responsibilities to Burton no longer required him to finish it, he also abandoned *Rodman* because he found a more interesting and creative way to retell the story of the American West: to tell it as the experience of a Norwegian fisherman caught within the Norway maelström; to tell it symbolically as a short tale, "A Descent into the Maelström."

The story marks a crucial point in Poe's development as a writer. Let others write romances of the American West; he would take Western images and motifs and layer them onto another story. "A Descent into the Maelström," after all, is not only a story of the American West, it is also an analogue of Old World and New, a parallel between enterprise and creative endeavor, an echo of Christ's life, and many other stories rolled into one. After adapting the Western imagery from *Rodman* for "A Descent into the

Maelström," Poe never attempted another book-length fictional narrative.

Poe completed his dissociation from both *Pym* and *Rodman* with his review of James Fenimore Cooper's *Wyandotté, or The Hutted Knoll*. Linking ocean voyages with journeys into the wilderness, Poe asserted that both settings generated such natural curiosity that "a failure might be properly regarded as conclusive evidence of imbecility on the part of the author. The two theses in question have been handled *usque ad nauseam* – and this through the instinctive perception of the universal interest which appertains to them. A writer, distrustful of his powers, can scarcely do better than discuss either one or the other. A man of genius will rarely, and should never, undertake either."[25] Poe never doubted his own genius; his suggestion that a man of genius would never undertake imaginative journeys detached him from the two longest creative works he had written.

In the review of Cooper's *Wyandotté*, Poe also revised his earlier opinion regarding *Robinson Crusoe*. The interest of such narratives, he explained, had "no reference to *plot*, of which, indeed, our novelist seems altogether regardless, or incapable, but depends, first, upon the nature of the theme; secondly, upon a Robinson-Crusoe-like detail in its management." A half-dozen years before Poe had elevated those narratives in which authors closely identified with their subjects, yet here he denigrates them as a "popular and widely circulated class" of literature "read with pleasure, but without admiration." Better novels, "not so popular, nor so widely diffused," achieve "a distinctive and highly pleasurable interest, springing from our perception and appreciation of the skill employed, of the genius evinced in the composition." He further explained, "After perusal of the one class, we think solely of the book – after reading the other, chiefly of the author. The former class leads to popularity – the latter to fame. In the former case, the books sometimes live, while the authors usually die; in the latter, even when the works perish, the man survives."[26]

When Edgar Allan Poe wrote the *Narrative of Arthur Gordon Pym*, he was hoping for both popular success and a lasting literary reputation. The *Journal of Julius Rodman* was written mainly as a magazine serial narrative, yet if completed it, too, could have been published in book form and might have contributed to its author's reputation. The commercial failure of *Pym* and Poe's dissatisfaction with *Rodman*, however, forced him to question seriously the worth of long narratives. He had hoped to write a work which would contribute to his contemporary reputation as well as create lasting fame, but, by the time he wrote the *Wyandotté* review, he came to realize the two were separate things. Popular taste and lasting fame seldom coincide. As Poe's career continued, he began to see the distinction not only in terms of different types of book-length narratives, but also in terms of literary genre. The novel, to Poe's understanding, was a passing thing written to satisfy the whims of the contemporary public. The short tale, on the other hand, could be a highly crafted work of art destined to withstand the ages.

CHAPTER 6

Poe's library

The richest minds need not large libraries.

– Bronson Alcott

Few things hinder the development of a fine private library more than poverty and restlessness. Though Edgar Allan Poe sometimes tried to keep his personal library intact from place to place through various turns of fortune, he never quite managed to do so. Returning to Richmond after leaving the University of Virginia, he brought his books with him. After quarrelling with John Allan, Poe left his Richmond home, yet he subsequently wrote to Allan multiple times, importuning him to send along the trunk containing his books.[1] A few years later, Poe reconciled his differences with Allan long enough to secure entrance to West Point. Packing for the military academy, Poe removed some books from the Allan home to take with him. An angry John Allan wrote to Cadet Poe, accusing him of purloining books not rightly his. Poe responded, "As to what you say about the books &c I have taken nothing except what I considered my own property."[2] Whatever books Poe had with him when he left West Point no doubt went the way of the secondhand shop during his lean years in Baltimore. He later told James Russell Lowell that he had not even kept copies of his first three volumes of poetry.[3]

When Poe joined the *Southern Literary Messenger*, he had the opportunity to accumulate a good collection of books for the first time in his life. After taking the position, he wrote to John P. Kennedy that he received from the publishers "nearly all new publications." The Harpers, for example, agreed to send him "all the works we publish – or at least such of them as are worthy of your notice."[4] It is difficult to say how many of the volumes Poe kept for his personal collection and how many he sold for ready cash. In the letter to Kennedy, Poe's reference to receiving new publications occurs immediately following a discussion of his salary at the *Messenger* and therefore implies that the books represented a salary supplement. The scant information which can be gleaned from Poe's surviving correspondence suggests he did not hold onto the volumes he received. Poe reviewed Frederick W. Thomas's first novel, *Clinton Bradshaw, or, The Adventures of a Lawyer*, for the *Southern Literary Messenger*, yet some years later he did not have a copy on hand. He and Thomas since had become good friends, and one morning Poe wrote to tell him that he was "going on a pilgrimage . . . to hunt up a copy of 'Clinton Bradshaw.'"[5] Perhaps Thomas had personally convinced Poe of the book's value. After his next novel, *Howard Pinckney*, appeared, Thomas wondered whether he preferred *Clinton Bradshaw* and told Poe, "[O]ur first book like our first love ever has the warmest place in our affections."[6] Though Poe may have kept a shelf of books in Richmond, the financial pressures marriage brought, exacerbated by a strong-willed mother-in-law who directly equated books with currency, assure us that most new volumes did not stay on Poe's shelf for long.

Poe may not have regretted the loss of these books too much, for few would have enhanced his personal library, in terms of either their outward appearance or the texts contained within. At the time Poe began writing for the *Messenger*, the book, as a physical object, was undergoing significant change. Cotton cloth had been introduced as a binding material only about ten years earlier. Before that, publishers generally issued books in paper-covered boards. These coverings were temporary ones designed to protect the stitched gatherings until the purchaser had time to take the volume to the bookbinder and have him prepare a fine leather binding. The book owner, not the publisher, assumed the cost of bookbinding. The introduction of muslin as a bookbinding material helped make edition binding possible, but the invention of the casing process more significantly reduced the labor costs of bookbinding and therefore convinced publishers to assume binding costs and begin issuing bound editions. The casing process allowed book covers to be assembled as separate units and then to be attached to the stitched and gathered sheets cheaply and quickly. Cased books and muslin bindings did not become commonplace until the mid-1830s, around the time Poe began writing for the *Southern Literary Messenger*.

In New York, the Harpers began using cloth bindings in the mid-1820s and were issuing cased books by 1831.[7] By 1836, the Harpers

had issued so many books bound in inexpensive muslin covers that
the firm practically became identified with them. When the Harpers
issued the sixth edition of Charles Anthon's *Sallust's Jugurthine War
and Conspiracy of Catiline* with a good quality binding, Poe found it
noteworthy:

In respect to external appearance this is an exceedingly beautiful book,
whether we look to the quality of its paper, the clearness, uniform color,
and great accuracy of its typography, or the neatness and durability of its
covering. In this latter point especially the Harpers and other publishers
would do well, we think, to follow up the style of the present edition of
Sallust – dropping at once and forever that flimsy and unsatisfactory
method of binding so universally prevalent just now, and whose sole
recommendation is its cheapness – if indeed it be cheaper at all . . . No
man of taste – certainly no lover of books and owner of a library – would
hesitate at paying twice as much for a book worth preservation, and which
there is some possibility of preserving, as for one of these fragile ephemera
which it is now the fashion to do up in muslin.[8]

Understanding Poe's pleasure with the Anthon binding and his
disgust with other contemporary cloth bindings requires knowledge
of one further technological innovation, the embossing process.
Embossing allowed manufacturers to give cotton cloth a variety of
textured patterns which greatly enhanced the aesthetics of the cloth-
bound book. The decorative embossing, which could make cloth
resemble the natural grain of morocco or the tooled patterns often
applied to calfskin, made it much easier for the book-buying public
to accept cloth bindings. Embossing, however, was not regularly
practiced in the American book industry until the late 1830s.[9] Even
after embossed cloth was introduced, some books continued to be
issued in unembossed muslin. Many editions were issued in a variety
of bindings. When the Harpers released the *Narrative of Arthur Gordon
Pym* in 1838, the work appeared with at least three different covers:
unembossed black muslin, black muslin embossed with a leafy
design, and blue cloth embossed with a textured pattern.[10]

Poe was reviewing books for the *Southern Literary Messenger* at a
unique time in the history of American book production, after
muslin-cased books had been adopted widely by the industry yet
before embossed cloth had become standard. His reaction to muslin
was shared by many bibliophiles of the time. Compared to hand-
crafted, elegantly gilt and tooled leather bindings, the unembossed
muslin looked exactly like what it was, a sign that books were

moving away from individual workmanship and toward mass production. In terms of look and feel, muslin bindings sacrificed aesthetic pleasure for utility, convenience, and thrift. If Poe had to give up muslin-bound books to make ends meet, it was not much of a sacrifice. Just as collectors nowadays refuse to shelf paperbacks among their fine books, bibliophiles in Poe's day were reluctant to allow muslin a place within their collections.

Lacking the natural texture and rich feel of leather, the muslin bindings offended the sense of touch, but their bright colors offended the discerning book-owner's sense of sight as well. Most leather bindings were somber-hued, but muslin greatly increased the variety of binding colors, and red, orange, and green books became commonplace. Shelved books began looking like the bands of a color spectrum. After its introduction, embossing would add texture and shadow to the cloth bindings and therefore mellow the colors, but, as a book reviewer in the mid 1830s, Poe often had to face books covered in brightly colored, unembossed muslin. And he did not like it. Green muslin particularly offended him.

In his critical notices for the *Southern Literary Messenger*, muslin bindings became a touchstone for mediocrity. Though Poe was not judging modern books by their covers, it did seem to him that such poor coverings did little to mask the banalities they contained. He called William L. Stone's *Ups and Downs* a "public imposition" in part due to its "customary muslin cover with a gilt stamp on the back."[11] Reviewing Lydia Maria Child's *Philothea*, a work he appreciated, Poe remarked, "Overwhelmed in a long-continued inundation of second-hand airs and ignorance, done up in green muslin, we turn to these pure and quiet pages with that species of gasping satisfaction with which a drowning man clutches the shore."[12] Poe does not describe the binding of his copy of *Philothea*, but the book was issued in at least three different colors of cloth – black, blue, purple – all fairly conservative and all decorated or embossed.[13]

Poe provided further thoughts on bookbinding in his highly favorable review of Augustus Baldwin Longstreet's *Georgia Scenes*. "Altogether this very humorous, and very clever book forms an aera in our reading," he wrote: "It has reached us per mail, and without a cover. We will have it bound forthwith, and give it a niche in our library as a sure omen of better days for the literature of the South."[14] *Georgia Scenes* was issued in tan paper boards, an old-fashioned binding for the muslin era. While suggesting that the work represented a bright future for Southern literature, Poe's treatment of the volume was reactionary, for he asserted that he would have the bookbinder prepare a handsome binding worthy of his private library. Good writing, Poe implied, deserved fine binding. There's no telling whether he had the volume bound or even held onto it, however. Even if he did not give *Georgia Scenes* a niche in his library, it held a niche in his memory. Ten years later Poe recalled Longstreet as the author "over whose inimitable 'Georgia Scenes' the whole continent has been laughing till the tears rolled from its eyes."[15]

In some ways, Poe's physical description of the *Georgia Scenes* volume was a fictional pose. It implied that he could afford to have rebound whatever books he felt worthy, which he could not. Furthermore, it suggested that he had a large personal library with room enough for a special niche, which he did not. Poe did recognize, however, that many of those who read the *Southern Literary Messenger* could afford fine bindings and did have large personal libraries. He once explained that the magazine's "subscribers [were] almost without exception the *élite*, both as regards wealth and intellectual culture, of the Southern aristocracy."[16] Thomas White sometimes ordered special books for his customers and occasionally served as a go-between with the local bookbinders. Beverley Tucker, for example, wrote to Poe, "I will thank you to ask Mr. White to procure me a copy of Burke's works as published in 1834, by Dearborn of New York, in three volumes. I wish him to have them lettered on the back near the bottom with the word Ardmore."[17] A young, poor, bookish man could only read these words with envy. Imagine not only being able to afford a three-volume edition of *The Works of Edmund Burke*, but also being able to have a bookbinder custom letter its spine. Tucker's lettering reinforced the association between a well-furnished home and shelves full of fine books.

Poe knew he could not afford a good library of his own, but he saw no reason for his readers to know. For the Longstreet review, he assumed the persona of a well-to-do gentleman who owned an excellent library. Poe would retain the persona throughout his editorial career. It gave him the authority to tell his audience what books they should or should not have in their libraries. Reviewing Eaton Stannard Barrett's *The Heroine, or Adventures of Cherubina*, for instance, Poe told his readers, "Cherubina is a book which should be upon the shelves of every well-appointed library."[18] At least one reader of Poe's "Literati of New York City" read the periodical series as an advice column recommending authors and works to purchase.[19]

Nowhere is Poe's persona of the well-to-do bookman more apparent than in the introduction to "Marginalia." T. O. Mabbott found the persona such an obvious fiction that he included it in his edition of Poe's short stories. The introduction begins, "In getting my books, I have been always solicitous of an ample margin; this not so much through any love of the thing in itself, however agreeable, as for the facility it affords me of pencilling suggested thoughts, agreements and differences of opinion, or brief critical comments in general." Supposedly, the random comments which follow present the texts of actual marginalia from books in Poe's library. He explains: "During a rainy afternoon, not long ago, being in a mood too listless for continuous study, I sought relief from *ennui* in dipping here and there, at random, among the volumes of my library – no very large one, certainly, but sufficiently miscellaneous; and, I flatter myself, not a little *recherché*."[20] Though the persona and the library are fictitious, the random and miscellaneous qualities do apply to Poe's reading process.

In other writings, Poe expressed his appreciation of fine book-bindings and his belief that a roomful of gilt and tooled volumes affected the reader reading there. Describing Charles Anthon's study, Poe explained that Anthon's "love of elegance" prompted him "to surround himself, in his private study, with gems of sculptural art and beautifully bound volumes, all arranged with elaborate attention to form, and in the very pedantry of neatness."[21] In "The Philosophy of Furniture," Poe imagined an ornately decorated yet sparsely furnished room. Among the few pieces of furniture are some "light and graceful hanging shelves, with golden edges and crimson silk cords and gold tassels, [which] sustain two or three hundred magnificently bound books."[22] "The Philosophy of Furniture" is a fantasy piece. The sketch tells how Poe might furnish a room if he could afford to do so. The "magnificently bound" books he describes show the effect book bindings could have on a room's appearance. Elegantly bound volumes standing upon a richly decorated hanging shelf could contribute as much to a room's ambience as the paper and paintings which also adorned its walls. Poe's imagination gave him a finer library than his income ever could.

Most of the books Poe managed to save from those he received in Richmond he would have sold in New York when he was unable to find employment in 1837. Poe was destined to repeat this accumulate-then-sell pattern time and again. He left New York for Philadelphia where his stint with *Burton's Gentleman's Magazine* gave him the chance to gather new publications which subsequent unemployment would have forced him to sell. His tenure with *Graham's Magazine* gave him another opportunity to accumulate books, yet his departure from *Graham's* led to further poverty and greater pressure to sell books in order to survive.

When Edgar and Virginia Poe moved to New York in 1844, they left Maria Clemm in Philadelphia to tie up loose ends before she joined them. In a letter written shortly after he and his wife reached New York City, Poe reminded Mrs. Clemm to return William Duane Jr.'s copy of a *Southern Literary Messenger* volume. Poe's friend Henry B. Hirst had borrowed it from Duane on Poe's behalf. The fact that Poe had to borrow a volume of the magazine he had contributed to and edited indicates how deeply poverty had eaten away at his library. Maria Clemm promptly sold the volume to a Philadelphia bookdealer. The practice of turning books in the family's possession into ready cash had become so commonplace that she thought nothing of selling the borrowed volume. Duane, a great grandson of Benjamin Franklin, was a keen bookman, however. He sorely missed the errant volume, and wrote Poe angry letters urging him to return it. Maria Clemm's insensitive act cost Poe no little bother. Only when Duane located his missing volume in Richmond did he realize, with great indignation, that it had been sold. After Poe's death, Duane joined those who impugned his character.[23]

Poe had an important journalistic opportunity in 1845 which he could not bypass. Given the chance to write for, to edit, and ultimately to own the *Broadway Journal* in 1845, Poe took it. Though the weekly journal fell far short of the ideal magazine he imagined, it could provide a good stepping stone for his journalistic ambitions, so Poe could not forgo the opportunity. After he began writing for the weekly journal, he borrowed money to buy a share of it and then borrowed more money to buy the journal outright. Poe's association with the *Broadway Journal* in 1845 gave him the best opportunity to acquire new publications since he had worked for the *Southern Literary Messenger* ten years before, though, with the added financial pressures ownership brought, few gratis volumes remained in his possession for long.

During his time with the *Broadway Journal*, Poe eventually realized the impossibility of an individual, even a wealthy individual, assembling a large collection of necessary books. He called for a serious public library:

When shall we have a permanent Library in New York? – not a Circulating Library, with the volume which you want somewhere, probably, between finger and thumb in Westchester county, but a library confined to the premises, with a perpetual writ of *ne exeat*, included in the charter, against all volumes leaving the front door. It is not necessary that the library should be so large as many of the century accumulations of Europe. Fifty thousand volumes on the spot would be sufficient – gathered together scientifically, in the first instance, with proportion and completeness for the departments. Pens, ink and paper, wide chairs and wide tables, should be added; attendants for convenience and care of the books; and some formality to check the mere literary loafers and all Collegians in round-a-bout jackets.[24]

The source of Poe's dissatisfaction is somewhat difficult to pinpoint. New York did have many ephemeral circulating libraries which catered to the novel-reading public, yet it also had the Society Library which had been founded nearly a century before. The New York Society Library held an excellent collection of books encompassing a wide range of knowledge. Furthermore, it was a serious collection which contained relatively few frivolous modern novels. In 1840, it had moved into a new building at the corner of Broadway and Leonard Street (where Poe would lecture three years later). Shortly after the new building opened, one visitor described it at length:

The New York Society Library has lately been re-opened in its new and beautiful edifice . . . a new ornament of our principal avenue. The basement floor is divided into stores and offices. A spacious hall occupies the middle of the building. The visitor enters this and ascends a broad flight of stairs, which leads to the reading room in the rear. This is a lofty and well proportioned apartment, with windows at each end, and in it are four commodious tables covered with rich food for the literary appetite. One contains the city journals; another those from different parts of the United States; and the other two are loaded with English and American periodicals – weekly, monthly and quarterly; literary, scientific, religious and political. This room, brilliantly lighted at night, with its soft carpets deadening the sound of footsteps, its cushioned arm chairs, and its rich supplies of periodicals, renewed by every steamship, forms the perfection of literary luxury. From a landing place upon the grand staircase two flights turn and ascend to the book room, which is a spacious apartment in the front of the building, with two rows of columns dividing it, and formed into alcoves by the cases which contain the books, arranged in double ranks. The librarian's desk faces the entrance. Connecting the reading room and the book room are two smaller apartments, used as conversation parlors, to avoid disturbing the readers, as committee rooms, and as studies for those authors who desire to pursue their investigations with their authorities around them, or who wish to make new books on old Burton's recipe, "as apothecaries make new mixtures, by pouring out of one vessel into another."[25]

Such luxury came at a cost. Poe could no more afford a share in the New York Society Library in 1845 than he could have afforded a share in the Library Company of Baltimore a dozen years before. As Austin Keep explained in his fine history of the Library, the expense of the shares and the fact that they were often handed down from one generation to the next gained for the New York Society Library the reputation as the library of New York society.[26]

When the *Broadway Journal* failed in early 1846, Poe's supply of free books ran dry. The loss was particularly painful, for, returning to his long-planned study of American literature after the journal's demise, Poe needed books more than ever. The financial pressures of running the magazine, combined with the domestic pressures created by his wife's illness and her domineering mother, forced Poe to convert his review copies to cash almost as soon as he had noticed them. An example: the penultimate issue of the *Broadway Journal* had noticed George Gilfillan's *Sketches of Modern Literature and Eminent Literary Men*, a work containing a section on Ralph Waldo Emerson which also discussed several other American authors. Resuming his study of American literature after the *Journal* folded, Poe needed the book, but he no longer had a copy and had to ask Evert Duyckinck if he could borrow his.[27]

To acquire more books, Poe was willing to pillage his collection of autographs, a collection which had cost him much time and effort to assemble. He wrote to Duyckinck, then working as editor for Wiley and Putnam's: "It strikes me that, some time ago, Wiley and Putnam advertised for autographs of distinguished Amer. statesmen. Is it so? I have well-preserved letters from John Randolph, Chief Justice Marshall, Madison, Adams, Wirt, Duane, E. Everett, Clay, Cass, Calhoun and some others – and I would exchange them for books."[28] Since this query occurs in a letter which asks for more autographs, those from many contemporary authors, it indicates that by this time, Poe was concentrating his literary study on living authors. He needed books, recent books, to write about living authors; he did not need autographs of men he no longer intended to write about. Poe's letter to Duyckinck verifies that his library was a working one, not a collection of rarities. After all, the autographs of well-known American statesmen were fine collectibles, yet Poe was willing to sacrifice them to acquire recently published books, items with little value as collectibles yet greatly useful for his literary purposes (and readily marketable once he was through with them).[29]

The publication of *Tales* in early 1845 and *The Raven and Other Poems* late that same year gave Poe the two most successful books of his career. He had multiple copies of each to present to friends and correspondents, and the Brownings and Charles Dickens were among the grateful recipients. Presenting copies of his own works to others, Poe began receiving copies from them. Among the handful of known volumes containing evidence of Poe's ownership are two presentation copies: Henry B. Hirst's *The Coming of the Mammoth, The Funeral of Time, and Other Poems* (Boston, 1845), inscribed, "To Edgar A. Poe, esq., with the regards of his friend Hirst, June, 1845," and Ralph Hoyt's *A Chaunt of Life, and Other Poems, with Sketches and Essays . . . Part II* (New York, 1845), inscribed "Edgar A. Poe Esq. with compliments of R. Hoyt, July 28th, 1845." A copy of Robert Browning's *Strafford; An Historical Tragedy*, inscribed and dated 15 June 1846, by Poe, survived into the twentieth century.[30]

Poe's correspondence shows that he acquired many other presentation copies. After editing Elizabeth Oakes Smith's *Poems*, John Keese gave Poe a copy of the edition.[31] Bayard Taylor sent him a copy of his *Views Afoot, Or Europe Seen with a Knapsack and Staff*, a work Poe found "picturesque and vigorous,"[32] and Maria McIntosh presented him with a copy of her collection of tales, *Two Lives, Or, To Seem and To Be*. The copy does not survive, but Poe's note of thanks verifies that she inscribed it for him because Poe wrote that the volume was made "doubly valuable by her autograph."[33] Presumably after receiving a copy of *Tales*, R. H. Horne responded in kind and offered Poe a copy of his play, *Cosmo De' Medici: An Historical Tragedy*, and a copy of the second British edition of August Wilhelm von Schlegel's *A Course of Lectures on Dramatic Art and Literature*, for which he had written the introduction.[34] An earlier edition of Schlegel may have been one of the few books Poe had held onto since his days with the *Southern Literary Messenger*, yet he would hardly have refused Horne's offer. Even Poe's presentation copies were not sacrosanct, however. He "had no very high opinion of the modern

generators of books, especially those so employed around him,"
William Gowans explained, "and hence many of these gifts found an
early transfer into the possession of some second-hand dealer at
wonderfully reduced prices."[35]

Poe moved his family to Fordham early in 1846. Though they
experienced little relief from their poverty, the pleasant cottage they
rented gave Poe more stability than he had known since his
adolescence in Richmond. Gowans wrote the best contemporary
description of Poe's modest library at the Fordham cottage. He
recalled that Poe "had a library made up of newspapers, magazines
bound and unbound, with what books had been presented to him
from time to time by authors and publishers."[36] After Poe had
returned to New York in 1844, he renewed his acquaintance with
Gowans, whose secondhand book business had continued to thrive.
Their friendship allowed Poe to browse Gowans's shelves at leisure,
even if he could not afford to purchase volumes they contained.
During the mid 1840s, Gowans had another customer destined for
literary fame whose ability to afford rare books was only slightly
better than Poe's. Around 1847, Herman Melville purchased a copy
of Robert Burton's *Anatomy of Melancholy* at Gowans's store.[37]
Imagine the author of "The Raven" and the author of *Typee* rubbing
shoulders amidst shelves redolent of old morocco.

Mary Neal Gove's description of Poe's library at Fordham is not
dissimilar to Gowans's. While visiting the Poe family, she noticed "a
light stand, and a hanging bookshelf . . . There were pretty presentation copies of books on the little shelves, and the Brownings had
posts of honour on the stand."[38] Gove's reference to a hanging
bookshelf is especially pleasing. In "The Philosophy of Furniture,"
Poe had imagined that an ideally furnished room would contain a
hanging bookshelf filled with finely bound volumes. Though he
could not afford quality bindings and though it seems unlikely that
his real hanging bookshelf had the gold edges of his imaginary one,
it is satisfying to learn that he partially realized his idea of the well-
furnished room.

Near the end of his life, Poe had the opportunity to furnish a
library to suit his taste. Marie Louise Shew, the well-to-do woman
who had nursed Virginia Poe through her final illness, invited Poe to
decorate her uncle's music room and library, and she gave him *carte
blanche* so to do.[39] He probably avoided placing a bust of Pallas
within the library – Elizabeth Barrett told him that an acquaintance

of hers who had read "The Raven" could no longer bear to look at her bust of Pallas in the twilight[40] – but as he designed the library, he no doubt combined elements from the fine private libraries he knew, especially those of Duyckinck and Anthon, and the libraries he had imagined for his fiction.

While Poe could not afford a home with a separate room filled with well-bound volumes, he never had trouble imagining one. His fiction is filled with fine libraries in ancestral homes. Among Poe's early stories, "Berenice" gives great importance to the private library. The story's narrator characterizes his family as a "race of visionaries" and explains that "the fashion of the library chamber" and "the very peculiar nature of the library's contents" exemplified their visionary qualities. The narrator personally identifies with the library; he was born there and spent much of his early life within its walls. During his upbringing, he had come to equate his entry into the library as a visit to "the very regions of fairy-land – into a palace of imagination – into the wild dominions of monastic thought and erudition."[41] Indeed, the imaginative world the library represents has affected him so profoundly that he loses the ability to discriminate between the imaginary and the real, a loss which has dire consequences for the story's title character.

In no other tale does Poe describe a character's books in more detail than he does in "The Fall of the House of Usher." The story's narrator associates Roderick Usher's personal character with the books he reads and then lists several book titles. Most of the listed books are either imaginary journeys or, at least, imaginative geographies. In *Iter Subterraneum*, for example, a work Thomas DeQuincey found enormously appealing, the great Danish writer, Baron Ludwig Holberg, takes his fictional narrator, Nicholas Klimm, on an imaginary voyage underground. In terms of his physical behavior, Usher never leaves the house and the slightest sensations greatly disturb him, yet his inability to travel beyond the confines of his home scarcely prevent his mind from wandering. At the time Poe wrote "The Fall of the House of Usher" his longest works had been imaginary voyages: "Hans Phaall" and the *Narrative of Arthur Gordon Pym*. Placing such voyages within Usher's library, Poe reinforced the significance of the imaginary world over the real. The books Usher reads allow him to use his imagination to travel through time and space and therefore obviate any need for physical travel.

In "The Sphinx," to cite one further example, the library of a

friend significantly affects the narrator's perception of reality. He
and his friend escape the pestilence of the city for a country home
where they have many books to amuse them. Surreptitiously reading
"certain volumes" he finds in his friend's library, the narrator is
forcibly impressed and falls into an "abnormal gloom." The books
he reads are "of a character to force into germination whatever
seeds of hereditary superstition lay latent in my bosom." He further
explains: "Near the close of an exceedingly warm day, I was sitting,
book in hand, at an open window, commanding, through a long vista
of the river banks, a view of a distant hill, the face of which nearest
my position, had been denuded, by what is termed a land-slide, of
the principal portion of its trees. My thoughts had been long
wandering from the volume before me to the gloom and desolation
of the neighboring city."[42] The book, in other words, leads to a new
way of perceiving the world. Succumbing to the library's influence,
the narrator transforms elements of actual topography and ento-
mology into a landscape of the mind.

In a way, it is a little sad to think that Poe, a man with such a
passionate interest in books who was such an important part of
America's literary scene, could never afford a good library of his
own; but we need not grieve for Poe. Perhaps if he had been able to
assemble a fine library, he would not have imagined such wonderful
ones as those in "The Philosophy of Furniture," "Berenice," "The
Fall of the House of Usher" and "The Sphinx." And our own
libraries would be the worse for it.

CHAPTER 7

Cheap books and expensive magazines

Literature is at a sad discount. There is really nothing to be done in this way. Without an international copyright law, American authors may as well cut their throats. A good magazine, of the true stamp, would do wonders in the way of a general revivication of letters, or the law. We must have – both if possible.

– Poe to Frederick W. Thomas, 27 August 1842

The cost-saving muslin bindings of the early-to-mid 1830s scarcely prepared Poe for the poorly printed and paper-covered pamphlet novels which would appear at the decade's end. New steam-powered papermaking and printing techniques combined with the lack of international copyright law allowed American publishers to issue mass quantities of popular British novels or English translations of French novels for pennies a copy. Introduced in the late 1830s, pamphlet novels, which looked more like magazines than books, proliferated during the early 1840s. These cheap books profoundly influenced the American publishing industry and significantly shaped the direction of Poe's literary career.

The pamphlet novel originated in the periodical press. In 1839, Rufus Griswold and Park Benjamin began editing the mammoth weekly, *Brother Jonathan*. Before the year's end, they turned the paper over to its publisher, Wilson and Company. The following year Griswold and Benjamin teamed up with Jonas Winchester to begin the *New World*. Like *Brother Jonathan*, the *New World* was a mammoth weekly, a large-format paper with pages as wide as four feet and containing some eleven columns. To fill their columns, these two mammoth papers began pirating and serializing British novels and English translations of Continental novels. With no international copyright restrictions, such literary piracy became commonplace. The editors of these weeklies ran into problems competing with book publishers, however, who also pirated British novels. Serial publication took time whereas the book publishers could rush a complete volume into print as soon as the first copies of the work to be pirated arrived from Europe. *Brother Jonathan* and the *New World* rose to the competition and began issuing complete novels as "extras." The publishers sent men to meet arriving steamships before they docked in order to obtain the earliest possible copies of the newest English novels. Employing numerous typesetters and working them all day and through the night, they could have a complete work set in type, printed, and on the streets within twenty-four hours.[1]

Closely printed in small type on inexpensive paper with multiple columns per page and issued in paper covers, these pamphlet novels reduced the triple-decker Victorian novel to a volume of perhaps thirty to seventy pages which sold from $6\frac{1}{4}$ cents to a quarter. During his second visit to the United States in the mid 1840s, British geologist Charles Lyell found that the same works which, in England, required a significant amount of money to purchase could be had for pennies in America. So many people read pamphlet novels that widespread ocular damage was feared. Lyell further wrote, "Many are of opinion that the small print of cheap editions in the United States, will seriously injure the eyesight of the rising generation, especially as they often read in railway cars, devouring whole novels, printed in newspapers, in very inferior type."[2] The remark reflects a common concern, but advantages in convenience and thrift permitted by these new formats countered fears of eye injury. As one contemporary American critic of cheap literature remarked, "[I]n this country, there are few words that have so attractive a sound as 'cheap.'"[3]

Sold on the street at news-stands and read in such public places as railway cars, pamphlet novels became part of the visual landscape. When Nathaniel Hawthorne noticed a train pulling into a small New England station, for example, he saw several passenger cars, each filled with people "reading newspapers, reading pamphlet novels, chatting, sleeping; all this vision of passing life!"[4] Their garish paper covers made pamphlet novels all the more noticeable in public. Evert Duyckinck called them the "crimson and yellow literature" – the "hues of blood and the plague."[5] One could scarcely walk through any crowded public place in the early 1840s without noticing these brightly covered pamphlets clutched in hand or tucked under arm and therefore being reminded of the ubiquity of foreign literature in America.

All the popular European authors of Poe's day made it into cheap American editions. Many of the sentimental, picaresque works of the French novelist, Charles-Paul de Kock, for example, were available in cheap English translations during the early 1840s. *Sister Anne* was published in 1843 as a *Brother Jonathan* extra. The following year, *The Six Mistresses of Pleasure* and *The Student's Girl* appeared in cheap editions. One vociferous opponent of cheap literature recalled its beginnings and harshly criticized the dissemination of such seemingly vulgar French literature: "Dumas, De Kock, and a hundred others, whose very brains ran to seed with their rank growth, were vomited forth ubiquitously in all parts of our land. The distorted, unreal, grotesquely horrible creations of perverted French taste, became as familiar as Robinson Crusoe."[6] A reference Poe made to De Kock in his fiction reflects his disgust with the popular French author whose works many American readers preferred over native productions. In "The System of Dr. Tarr and Professor Fether," Poe named one of the lunatics "De Kock": the one who brays like a donkey.

Another of Poe's references to a popular foreign author whose works were widely available in cheap American reprints is more subtle. William Harrison Ainsworth, a contemporary British writer, enjoyed much popularity among American readers. Finding Ainsworth's *Crichton* less than admirable, Poe called it "a somewhat ingenious admixture of pedantry, bombast, and rigmarole."[7] Several of Ainsworth's books were available as pamphlet novels. *The Miser's Daughter* appeared as a *Brother Jonathan* extra in 1842. *Windsor Castle, An Historical Romance* appeared as a *New World* extra in 1843, and *Modern Chivalry, or, A New Orlando Furioso* appeared as a *New World* extra in January 1844. For the "Balloon Hoax," published just a few months after the cheap edition of *Modern Chivalry* appeared, Poe made Ainsworth one of the men who crosses the ocean from England to America. While the presence of a real-life author aboard the ocean-crossing balloon is usually interpreted as another device contributing to the story's *vraisemblance*, the fact that the author specified is Ainsworth (instead of, say, Charles Dickens) makes the story a comment on the swiftness with which mediocre British literature made its way to America. Much of the narrative is told in the form of a journal by Monck Mason, another real-life persona who is the balloon's inventor in the story. Ainsworth's remarks appear as postscripts to Mason's daily entries. The relationship of their written comments in the story conveys Poe's idea of the proper relationship between the two. The popular writer should be sub-servient to the creative genius.

American authors seldom complained about being outsold by pirated editions of Scott or Dickens, but as mediocre British writers became more widely read in America than the finest native writers, the locals had reason to complain. Poe came to believe that the absence of international copyright law rendered it nearly impossible for American authors to be remunerated for their literary labors.[8] He directly linked the pamphlet novel – "the external insignificance of the yellow-backed pamphleteering" – to the lack of international copyright law.[9] In his private correspondence and published wri-tings, Poe frequently decried the lack of copyright laws and recog-nized the damage done to native authors.

While British and translated French books could be had in cheap editions in the United States, the opposite phenomenon took place in Great Britain where American books were pirated and published cheaply. John Cunningham, a Fleet Street publisher, issued several pamphlet novels printed two columns to the page and known collectively as the "Novel Newspaper" series. Most were reprints of pirated American novels. The series was intended as a deliberate counter-campaign against American piracy of British texts, as the publisher admitted in some prefatory remarks to one of several James Fenimore Cooper works. Besides Cooper, the series included many works written by Poe's friends, acquaintances, and kindred spirits: Robert M. Bird's *Hawks of Hawk-Hollow*, Charles Brockden Brown's *Wieland*, John Pendleton Kennedy's *Horse-Shoe Robinson* as well as his *Rob of the Bowl*, Caroline Kirkland's *A New Home*, John Neal's *Logan, the Mingo Chief*, James Kirke Paulding's *Koningsmarke*, and William Gilmore Simms's *Confession, or The Blind Heart*. Michael Sadleir lists all of these titles in his excellent study of nineteenth-century fiction. He does not mention one additional title, however, which Cunningham added to the series in 1841: *Arthur Gordon Pym: Or, Shipwreck, Mutiny, and Famine*.[10] Cunningham's revised title emphasized the most sensational qualities of Poe's work and thus made it all the more suitable for the cheap print trade.

Other Poe works were also pirated and issued in cheap British editions. "The Facts of M. Valdemar's Case," a work Philip Pen-dleton Cooke called "the most damnable, vraisemblable, horrible, hair-lifting, shocking, ingenious chapter of fiction that any brain ever conceived,"[11] appeared in the *American Review* in late 1845, and some took it for a genuine example of mesmerism. Short and Co., a London firm, pirated the work and reprinted it as *Mesmerism "in articulo mortis": An Astounding and Horrifying Narrative, Shewing the Extraordinary Power of Mesmerism in Arresting the Progress of Death*, a sixteen-page pamphlet which sold for threepence. "The Gold-Bug" also appeared as a cheap London pamphlet. Published by A. Dyson, who generally published pamphlets treating contemporary economic issues, *The Gold Bug* was the first number of what Dyson projected to be a lengthy series, "The Thousand-and-One Romances." Using *The Gold Bug* to lead off a literary series, Dyson revealed his confidence in the strength of Poe's work among British readers. The failure of the series suggests that Dyson may have been more forward-thinking than the British reading public. To my knowledge, "The Thousand-and-One Romances" began and ended with *The Gold Bug*.[12]

Respectable publishers who issued the works of native authors needed a way to compete with the pirated imports. Yet there was no way they could honor contracts, pay royalties, and still publish book-length works at prices which could compete with the cheap books. The commercial success of the pamphlet novel helped perpetuate the long-standing practice of publishing a long work in separate parts. This part-by-part publishing had taken place for some decades, and one of the most famous books in American literature, Washington Irving's *The Sketch Book of Geoffrey Crayon*, appeared in parts in 1819 and 1820. The idea was that once consumers had acquired all the parts, they could have them handsomely bound together as a single volume which would make a fine addition to their personal libraries. The publishing industry's eventual adaptation of edition binding should have tolled the death knell for part-by-part book publication during the early 1830s, but the competition created by the pamphlet novels helped perpetuate it through the 1840s.

In 1843, Philadelphia publisher William H. Graham issued *The Prose Romances of Edgar A. Poe*, a 48-page pamphlet containing "The Murders in the Rue Morgue" and "The Man that Was Used Up" which sold for $12\frac{1}{2}$ cents. The work was published as part of Poe's "Uniform Serial Edition," the first of several numbers planned.[13] A collection of Poe's stories published part-by-part, Graham realized, had an advantage over novels similarly published, for each part could be complete in itself. The Philadelphia papers noticed the pamphlet and looked forward to the finished volume. The *Pennsylvania Inquirer*, for example, noticed the publication "with sincere pleasure, an undertaking which will collect his admirable stories together, and afford the public an opportunity of possessing them in a convenient form," and the *Saturday Evening Post* stated that once completed the edition would make "a very handsome volume."[14] The edition was never completed, however. That same year William H. Graham tried his hand at pamphlet publication again with a cheap edition of Henry William Herbert's *Ringwood the Rover, A Tale of Florida*, but no more Poe pamphlets followed.[15] Graham relocated to New York where he continued to publish cheap books and also acted as a magazine agent.

To Poe's mind, the pamphlet novels brought the book to a new low. Not only did it represent the publishers' deliberate efforts to undercut American authors by making foreign literature much more affordable than American, it also made the book, as a material object, a loathsome thing, a disposable commodity. With its hard-to-read type and garish paper covers, the cheap book made even unembossed muslin-bound volumes seem like models of good bookmanship. While the relationship between the *Journal of Julius Rodman* and "A Descent into the Maelström" indicates Poe's preference for the short story over the book-length narrative, his aesthetic inclinations only partially explain his personal aversion to the book-length narrative. The very real circumstances surrounding book production and publication around the time he wrote "A Descent into the Maelström" convinced Poe that book publishing held little hope for native authors.

Though he disliked the pamphlet novel, Poe nevertheless learned a lesson from it, for he recognized the allure of its convenience and portability. The pamphlet novel and the passenger railway, both results of steam technology, signaled the increasing pace of American society. People wanted books they could carry with them and read on the go. In a letter to Washington Irving, Poe predicted, "The brief, the terse, the condensed, and the easily circulated will take place of the diffuse, the ponderous, and the inaccessible."[16] As the medium of cheap print turned a book-length work into a pamphlet, it condensed the size of type and the amount of white space per page. The pamphlet novel physically condensed text; Poe's approach was much different, for he wrote stories which condensed much meaning into as few words as possible. The pamphlet novel, though a different medium, presented the same text as a full-length hardcover book. The medium changed yet the text did not. Poe believed that a different medium was necessary – the magazine. He came to believe that owning and editing a magazine offered the best way for him to determine the course of American literature.

Not just any magazine would do, however. It had to be an expensive, high-quality magazine. In Poe's day, there were three grades of monthly magazine – dollar magazines, three-dollar magazines, and five-dollar magazines, the price referring to the cost of a one-year subscription. For Poe, only a five-dollar magazine would do. In 1843, James Russell Lowell had attempted a three-dollar magazine, the *Pioneer*, which Poe received and contributed to, yet it failed miserably and folded after only three issues. Lowell's experience gave Poe an object lesson in magazine editing. When a correspondent suggested that he undertake a three-dollar magazine, Poe told him he could not undertake it *con amore*. His heart would not be in it. The mere idea of a three-dollar magazine, he continued, "would suggest namby-pambyism and frivolity."[17] As Poe recognized, three-dollar magazines lacked a clear audience, for they attempted to suit readers of popular literature as well as discriminating readers. Poe wrote, to a potential collaborator, "Experience, not less than the most mature reflection on the topic, assures me that no *cheap* Magazine can ever again prosper in America. We must aim high – address the intellect – the higher classes – of the country (with reference, also, to a certain amount of foreign circulation) and put the work at $5."[18] A single issue of his five-dollar magazine would cost more than three average pamphlet novels. Twice a year, the separate issues could be gathered together and nicely bound to make a fine addition to anyone's personal library. In modern times, books get saved while magazines are pitched, but in the era of the pamphlet novel, Poe imagined a magazine which would be worth keeping while cheap books fell by the wayside.

Poe saw a clear correlation between the quality of the printed page and the text it contained and devoted much thought to the physical appearance of his planned magazine. Among the finer periodicals, he had several possibilities on which to model his own. Even before he began working for the *Southern Literary Messenger*, he paid close attention to magazine page layouts. In a letter to Thomas White, he wrote, "I have heard it suggested that a lighter-faced type in the headings of your various articles would improve the appearance of the Messenger. Do you not think so likewise?"[19] His experience with the *Southern Literary Messenger* allowed him a good opportunity to compare the appearance of many different magazines. Elitist quarterlies such as the long-standing *North American Review* or the more recent *Southern Quarterly Review* and *New York Review*, had generous leading, ample margins, and large, easy-to-read typefaces. It seems unlikely Poe would have patterned his magazine after the *North American Review*, however, for he saw it as the official organ of Frogpondium, a staid and stuffy journal scarcely worth the paper on which it was printed. Poe once advised Nathaniel Hawthorne to throw all his odd numbers of the *North American Review* "out of the window to the pigs."[20]

The *North American Review* was patterned or, to use Poe's words, "slavishly and pertinaciously modelled" after the British quarterlies,[21] yet American readers in Poe's day generally did not know the British journals in their original editions, for they, too, were pirated and reprinted in the United States, and their physical appearance changed significantly in the inexpensive American editions. By 1835, New York publisher Theodore Foster had begun pirating and republishing four leading British reviews: *Edinburgh Review*, *Foreign Quarterly Review*, *Quarterly Review* (which he renamed the *London Quarterly Review*), and *Westminster Review*. Later, New York publisher Leonard Scott issued American editions of the same quarterlies and also published *Blackwood's Edinburgh Magazine*. The pirated American reprints were printed in a double-column format on large paper in small print with much less white space per page. The format change, however, little mattered to thrifty American readers. Foster and Scott offered customers a further discount if they purchased the first four titles together. Though Poe would later deride these pirated reprints in "Some Secrets of the Magazine Prison-House," he was impressed with them at first. Reviewing one issue of the *London Quarterly Review* during the 1830s, he remarked, "We take this opportunity of noticing the excellent American Edition of the London, Edinburgh, Foreign and Westminster Reviews, combined. It does much honor to Mr. Foster of New York, the publisher; and the compression of matter is such, without being printed too fine, as to give to subscribers for the sum of eight dollars, these four periodicals for which upwards of twenty dollars was formerly paid. The paper, type, and execution, are good."[22]

In terms of appearance, the *Southern Literary Messenger* most resembled the American editions of the British quarterlies. It, too, was printed in fine type and double columns. Poe initially believed the format represented good value. Reviewing a 200-page book printed in a large typeface with generous white spaces on the page which sold for a dollar, Poe suggested that one issue of the *Southern Literary Messenger* could contain the texts of six such books, all for around forty cents.[23] As Poe imagined his magazine, he tried to strike a balance between good value and ease of reading, between the crowded double-column pages of the pirated British quarterlies and the leisurely appearance of the American quarterlies.

As he planned his own monthly journal, which he decided to call the *Penn Magazine*, Poe foresaw that it would "nearly resemble" the *Knickerbocker*. In so saying, Poe defined specific guidelines for his magazine's physical appearance. The page layout of the *Knickerbocker* fell between that of the British quarterlies and their American reprints. Patterning his proposed magazine after the *Knickerbocker*, Poe imagined a printed page with a single column, yet with much smaller type and less generous leading than the American quarterlies. Poetry and prose would appear in the same-sized type, so the two would share equal importance. After the *Penn Magazine* was delayed, Poe had second thoughts about the format, and temporarily reverted to double columns for prose: "I am resolved upon a good outward appearance – clear type, fine paper &c – double columns, I think, and brevier, with the poetry running across the page in a single column."[24] Poe never proposed publishing poetry in double columns. When he submitted "The Bells" for publication in the last year of his life, he insisted upon its appearing in single columns.[25] ("The Bells" appeared posthumously – in double columns.) Once he reconceived the *Penn Magazine* as the *Stylus*, he settled on single columns for both poetry and prose.

Poe also devoted considerable thought to illustrations for his magazine. By and large, he reacted against magazines such as *Graham's* which included "contemptible pictures, fashion-plates, music and love tales" or, in other words, material which catered to female readers. Condemning its inclusion of steel-engraved fashion plates, Poe used the phrase "namby-pamby" to characterize *Graham's Magazine*, the same phrase he had used to describe the three-dollar magazines in general. The three-dollar magazines attempted to suit different classes, and *Graham's* tried to appeal to both sexes. For Poe, a namby-pamby magazine was one which sought to appeal to different kinds of reader, yet ultimately suited none. Poe believed that a magazine's editor and proprietor needed to target a specific audience and shape the magazine accordingly. By no means was Poe excluding female readers. Rather, he was appealing to readers, both men and women, who were interested in serious, high-quality literature, not in such frivolities as those found in *Graham's*.

Illustrations, Poe decided, should be used sparingly and only when necessary to illuminate the text. In a moment of great confidence, he wrote, "We *shall* make the most magnificent Magazine as regards externals, ever seen. The finest paper, bold type, in single column, and superb wood-engravings (in the manner of the French illustrated edition of 'Gil Blas' by Gigoux, or 'Robinson Crusoe' by Grandville)."[26] Poe soon enlisted the services of F. O. C. Darley to illustrate and went so far as to have him sign a contract. Darley, whom Poe praised as a "*genius* of a high order,"[27] would establish his reputation as the finest book illustrator in antebellum America, but when he signed the contract with Poe, he had yet to establish his reputation fully. In other words, Poe was among the first to recognize Darley's abilities.

Poe attempted to establish the *Penn Magazine* in 1840, and, to that end, he published a *Prospectus* describing its potential appearance and content. Unable to obtain sufficient financial support, he postponed his plans. Early in 1841 he became an editor for *Graham's Magazine* and, under his editorial guidance, *Graham's* more than quadrupled its subscriptions. With that success, Poe revived his plans for the *Penn Magazine*. In 1843, he changed the title of his proposed magazine to the *Stylus*, but, in terms of the format and content, Poe imagined it essentially the same. His public comments echo similar remarks he had made privately to Frederick W. Thomas. In the *Prospectus*, Poe wrote, "The late movements on the great question of International Copy-Right, are but an index of the universal *disgust* excited by what is quaintly termed the *cheap* literature of the day: – as if that which is utterly worthless in itself, can be cheap at any price under the sun."[28] Though still unable to gain financial backing for a magazine of his own, Poe continued plans for the *Stylus*. In 1844, he moved from Philadelphia to New York where, the following year, he became editor and proprietor of the *Broadway Journal*, which he hoped would be a stepping stone for his ideal magazine, but the project put him in deeper financial straits, and it failed with the first issue of 1846. Though his series of biographical and critical sketches, "The Literati of New York City," occupied much of his time in 1846, he never lost sight of the *Stylus* which he called "the grand purpose of my life, from which I have never swerved for a moment."[29] In January 1848, he published a new prospectus for the *Stylus* and another the following month. In the summer of 1849, Poe left New York intending to travel south through Richmond and then west to Saint Louis in order to generate support for the magazine. He would never return.

CHAPTER 8

The road to 'Literary America'

The book itself is curious, being a collection of spleen, critical acumen, excellent writing, brilliant metaphor, and poetical association seldom found together in the same pages.
– Thomas Powell, reviewing Poe's *Literati* (1850)

Besides founding and editing a first-class magazine, Edgar Allan Poe's other great ambition during the last decade of his life was to write a book-length survey of American literature. He partially realized the project in his series of periodical essays, "The Literati of New York City," but he never brought the whole thing to completion. Poe conceived the work over a period of several years. His early reading started him thinking about literary history and reminiscences. His chirographic analysis allowed him to indulge in literary gossip and personal criticism. Even after he decided to write a book-length work about American literature, the project changed course several times, but the various approaches coalesced, and Poe's last conception of the work combined biography, personal criticism, and literary analysis. The last title he came up with was *Literary America*. The earlier titles he imagined indicate the different directions taken by the project.

Poe's interest in literary history can be traced at least as far back as 1826, the year he spent at the University of Virginia where his attention to both history and literature may have given him the idea of writing a literary history. The University library allowed him the opportunity to read systematically, as his attention to history-reading indicates. Though Poe read voraciously throughout his life, his reading became more random after he left the University. In other words, never again would he have the opportunity to choose a subject and then read several major books relevant to that subject in succession. Instead, Poe read books as they came to him. As an editor, he read widely, yet the only pattern his reading followed was the publication order of the books he reviewed.

Other early reading may have influenced Poe's attitude toward literary biography. Reviewing Augustus Baldwin Longstreet's *Georgia Scenes*, Poe recalled the long-standing tradition of character-writing and suggested, "In regard, especially, to that class of southwestern mammalia who come under the generic appellation of 'savagerous wild cats,' he is a very Theophrastus in duodecimo. But he is not the less at home in other matters. Of geese and ganders he is the La Bruyère."[1] Poe's offhand references suggest his familiarity with Theophrastus' *Notationes morum*, which he may have read in his adolescence at Joseph Clarke's Richmond school. Poe also knew the work of Theophrastus' seventeenth-century editor, Jean de La Bruyere, who added many new sketches in his edition of Theophrastus' *Characters, or The Manners of the Age*. Poe's critical dictum that the death of a beautiful woman made the most appropriate artistic subject may owe a debt to La Bruyère, who wrote that a beautiful face was the most beautiful of sights. These writers gave Poe a pattern to follow, yet the biographical sketches he would write do not follow the traditional pattern of characters. Instead of describing specific personality-types, Poe sought to characterize real people important to American literature. Furthermore, his sketches lack the polish and structure of traditional character sketches. The essays he completed for his study of American literature have a rough, catch-as-catch-can quality. Nevertheless, Poe's eventual decision to subdivide his work into brief sections, each devoted to a single author without additional narrative to connect them, and his emphasis on the personal characteristics of his subjects reveal his debt to the character-writers.

At the *Southern Literary Messenger*, Poe also had the chance to read many memoirs and reminiscences, and these helped shape the direction of his literary study, too. Reviewing B. B. Thatcher's *Traits of the Tea Party*, for example, Poe wrote, "Reminiscences such as the present cannot be too frequently laid before the public. *More than anything else* do they illustrate that which can be properly called the History of our Revolution – and in so doing how vastly important do they appear to the entire cause of civil liberty?"[2] Reminiscences could capture the flavor of the times in a way which historians of times past could not. Similarly, Poe saw John Quincy Adams's personal recollections gave his *Jubilee of the Constitution* value: "What

Mr. Adams has thus done could not be so well done, perhaps, by any man living. The circumstances by which he has been surrounded from his boyhood – his intimate connexion, private and public, with the leading men of the Revolution – his long continued political career – his industrious habits of observation – his personal identification for nearly half a century with the interests of his subject – all had conspired to assure us that this subject would be skillfully handled, and the discourse itself assures us that, essentially it is."[3] Poe found Adams's discussion of the private world of the founding fathers especially worthwhile. His appreciation of Thatcher and Adams shows that he preferred personal reminiscence over historical reconstruction. This perference would shape his approach to writing literary history.

The *Autobiography* of Benvenuto Cellini reinforced the value Poe attached to reminiscences. Not only was autobiography useful for understanding the lives of writers, it also helped readers understand the times in which they lived and the people they knew. Reviewing a new edition of Cellini's *Autobiography*, Poe stated that the author's intimacy "with all the noted men of his very remarkable age" and his contact with the day's intrigues, both great and petty, made his book worth reading in later times. Cellini "felt keenly – in fact his excessive sensibility amounted to madness – and he has depicted his feelings, not less than his thoughts and deeds, with a hand of a profound moral painter."[4] The personal slant Cellini put on the men and manners of his time gave Poe a precedent for his own personal interpretation of the men and manners of mid nineteenth-century America. Poe's description of Cellini's work could almost be applied to his own, for the literary sketches he completed describe the notable writers of his day as well as their contact with the day's petty intrigues.

Poe knew well Isaac Disraeli's works: *Amenities of Literature, Curiosities of Literature,* and *Miscellanies of Literature.* He referred to Disraeli multiple times and plundered his works to fill the odd corners of magazines he edited. Disraeli showed Poe that a work of literary history need not be organized chronologically to have value. As Poe stated, the contents of Disraeli's *Miscellanies* – facts, anecdotes, literary legends, and miscellaneous information – were "marshalled together here in disorderly array, pushing, jostling, and crowding each other until they remind one of Falstaff's valorous regiment, or a militia training in a midland county," yet they nevertheless embodied "a vast amount of out-of-the-way intelligence, interesting to the general, but absolutely necessary to the literary reader."[5] Poe's individual essays in "The Literati of New York City" would follow no particular order. As he would explain, "As any precise order or arrangement seems unnecessary and may be inconvenient, I shall maintain none. It will be understood that, without reference to supposed merit or demerit, each individual is introduced absolutely at random."[6] The random order not only shows Disraeli's influence, it also reflects the random quality of Poe's own acquisition of knowledge.

"AUTOGRAPHY"

The first article Poe wrote that anticipated his "Literary America" project was the two-part "Autography." He drafted it in or before September 1835 and published it in the *Southern Literary Messenger* the following year.[7] "Autography" allowed Poe to do what he had largely avoided doing in his critical notices. Taking his reviewer's task seriously, Poe had avoided personal criticism for the most part in the *Southern Literary Messenger* reviews. In "Autography," however, he conveyed his personal impressions of many contemporary authors within a fictional framework. Fiction gave him more freedom to combine criticism with literary burlesque, something he had planned to do for the "Tales of the Folio Club." The deliberate fiction gave him the freedom to provide his opinions about many contemporary authors while standing behind a persona. The article was broken down into short sections. After a made-up letter attributed to a real author came a facsimile reproduction of his or her autograph, a brief analysis of the writer's chirography, another letter, and so on. The fictional premise of "Autography," however, did not sufficiently mask the truth behind it. After all, the autographs included as part of the article were well-executed woodcut facsimiles of real signatures of many authors known to the American reading public. All were living save Chief Justice Marshall, who had died in July 1835, and William Wirt, who had died the year before. The critical comments, though told from the point of view of a literary persona, often came too close to the truth for comfort. About Washington Irving, Poe wrote, "Mr. Irving's hand writing is common-place. There is nothing indicative of genius about it."[8] Though directed at Irving's handwriting, there can be little doubt that Poe was attacking his published writings as well. "Autography" represents Poe's first attempt to use a personal attribute to discern a writer's character. In the "Literati" essays, he would use a different personal attribute – physiognomy – in much the same way that he used handwriting in "Autography."

"A CHAPTER ON AUTOGRAPHY"

Writing for *Graham's Magazine* in late 1841 and early 1842, Poe contributed three more articles presenting and analyzing the autographs of prominent American authors. These articles, known collectively under the general title, "A Chapter on Autography," differed from the earlier "Autography" in several ways. First, Poe dropped the fictional pretense and excluded the made-up letters. "A Chapter on Autography" consists of a series of autographs, again reproduced in woodcut, each of which is followed by a discussion. In general, the discussions are lengthier than those in "Autography," and they often go well beyond analyzing the signature. Many provide biographical facts and indulge in literary gossip. The first item, describing Charles Anthon, fills nearly three pages in a modern edition. Prior to analyzing Anthon's handwriting, Poe gave a brief biography and mentioned his subject's remarkable scholarly accomplishments. Discussing Anthon's chirography, Poe wrote a virtual treatise on the scholarly life. In the third item, he described Park Benjamin's writing style *before* he analyzed his handwriting. Clearly, Poe no longer felt it necessary to disguise his critique of an author's writing style as a critique of his chirography. By the time he finished the three-article series, Poe realized that his ambition was outstripping his format. He wanted to do more than the autography approach would let him. He continued to believe in the importance of chirography and hoped to include autographs in *Literary America*, but he began considering new ways to treat American authors.

A CRITICAL HISTORY OF AMERICAN LITERATURE

Among Poe's surviving letters, the earliest indication that he had begun a book-length study of American literature occurs in a letter to James Russell Lowell written in mid-1844. He explained, "For myself I am very industrious – collecting and arranging materials for a Critical History of Am. Literature."[9] Though the idea of a body of written works which together formed a distinct American literature was at least as old as White Kennett's *Bibliothecae americanae primordia* (1713), few had attempted to chronicle the history of American literature. The fullest effort to date was Samuel Knapp's *Lectures on American Literature* (1829). In Poe's day, the prevailing impulse was to anthologize. From Samuel Kettell's pioneering three-volume *Specimens of American Poetry with Critical and Biographical Notes* (1829), many compilers brought together collections of American poetry. During the half-dozen years before Poe began his *Critical History*, there had been several collections of American verse. In 1839, John Keese published *The Poets of America*. The following year, George P. Morris compiled *American Melodies; Containing a Single Selection from the Productions of Two Hundred Writers*, and William Cullen Bryant edited *Selections from the American Poets*. Few of these anthologies contained critical or historical commentary; for the most part, they were giftbooks. The most important work on American literature to appear in the early 1840s was Rufus Griswold's *Poets and Poetry of America: With a Historical Introduction*. Griswold went beyond the role of mere compiler to provide much biographical information and critical interpretation. Poe admired the scope of Griswold's work yet thought he could do better himself. Poe's first published review of Griswold's work was fairly kind, but, privately, he was more severe. He wrote to a fellow editor, "Have you seen Griswold's Book of Poetry? It is a most outrageous humbug, and I sincerely wish you would 'use it up.'"[10]

After the appearance of Griswold's work and his own generous review, Poe felt the need to make his private opinions about the book public and, furthermore, to voice his general impressions of American poetry. Before he conceived the book-length *Critical History*, his first impulse was to go on tour and lecture about American poets and poetry. The impulse is understandable, for, after all, giving lectures, a popular form of bourgeois entertainment, was generally more lucrative than writing books and often provided a more effective forum for disseminating ideas than the printed word. Poe began lecturing in November 1843 and continued lecturing sporadically over the next few months. In general, his lectures were warmly received and his insights appreciated. The *Pennsylvania Inquirer* called Poe's Philadelphia lecture "one of the most brilliant and successful of the season."[11] He surveyed the various anthologies of American poetry and commented on each, expressed his frustration with Griswold's work, and recited much poetry. Poe eventually realized that though his public appearances could reach a wide segment of the American population, they could not reach the British. During the 1843–1844 lecture season, he recognized the importance of spreading his message across the Atlantic, something best done in print.

The main impetus for Poe's *Critical History* was an article which appeared in the January 1844 issue of the *Foreign Quarterly Review*. A lengthy review-essay treated Griswold's *Poets and Poetry of America* and discussed four separate books of verse including Longfellow's *Voices of the Night* and Bryant's *Poems*. Poe referred to the essay as "the slashing article in the Foreign Quarterly upon American poets which so much excited the ire of the newspapers."[12] Since Griswold had included a Poe section in his anthology, the reviewer took the opportunity to comment: "Poe is a capital artist after the manner of Tennyson; and approaches the spirit of his original more closely than any of them."[13] Poe found the comments uninformed. The examples of Poe's verse the reviewer quoted, after all, were written before Tennyson published the bulk of his work. Poe admitted that the reviewer told much truth about the state of American literature, yet he found that he also revealed "much ignorance and more spleen." Like most essays which appeared in the British quarterlies, this one was unsigned. Poe became convinced that Charles Dickens had written it and continued to assert his belief privately in his letters and publicly in the pages of the *Broadway Journal*.[14] James Russell Lowell suggested to Poe that the article had been written by Dickens's friend John Forster, who was also a friend to Longfellow and his circle.[15] Lowell's suggestion Poe found unconvincing. Poe believed Dickens had written the article because many of its opinions coincided with opinions Dickens had expressed to Poe personally during his visit to the United States in 1842. Poe continued to have great respect for Dickens, but the more he thought about the *Foreign Quarterly* article, the less he liked it. He found the "arrogance, ignorance and self-glorification of the Quarterly, with its gross injustice towards everything un-British . . . *mal-à-propos* in a journal exclusively devoted to foreign concerns, and therefore presumably imbued with something of a cosmopolitan spirit."[16]

The *Foreign Quarterly* was reprinted in the United States by the end of January 1844, and Park Benjamin reprinted the article separately in the *New World*. Poe must have decided to begin the *Critical History* soon after he read the article, for by the second half of 1844, he wrote to one correspondent that he had been hard at work on the project for seven or eight months. Around the same time, he confided to another that he was "in strict seclusion, busied with books and ambitious thoughts."[17]

In his correspondence, Poe expressed his wish to publish his *Critical History* in Great Britain as well as the United States. A surviving manuscript fragment of *Literary America* best indicates the audience Poe sought. In the essay, Poe characterized Thomas Dunn English, whom he refers to as Thomas Dunn Brown: "Were I writing merely for American readers, I should not, of course, have introduced Mr Brown's name in this book. With us, *grotesqueries* such as 'The Aristidean' and its editor, are not altogether unparalleled, and are sufficiently well understood – but my purpose is to convey to foreigners some idea of a condition of literary affairs among us, which otherwise they might find it difficult to comprehend or to conceive."[18] Not only does the passage clarify Poe's intended audience, it also clarifies Poe's intended purpose. He sought to inform British readers about the true state of letters in the United States. Instead of coating it with jingoist rhetoric, Poe wanted to give British readers a clear picture of literature in America, telling them what was notable without omitting its shortcomings.

AMERICAN PARNASSUS

Suggesting to Poe that John Forster wrote the *Foreign Quarterly* article, James Russell Lowell explained, "Forster is a friend of some of the Longfellow clique here which perhaps accounts for his putting L. at the top of our Parnassus."[19] The term "Parnassus," of course, refers to the mountain in Greece held sacred to the Muses, yet Lowell gives it a more local connotation. His use of the term was not unusual within the literary community. Poe may have picked it up from common usage or Lowell may have sparked the idea. Poe was also familiar with Traiano Boccalini's *Advices from Parnassus*.[20] Anyway, he soon made the term his own and changed the title of his planned work to *American Parnassus*. The title change indicates a significant shift in Poe's approach to the work. The earlier title *A Critical History of American Literature*, suggests that Poe sought to examine American literature across time, from its beginnings to the present day. The title *American Parnassus*, on the other hand, implies temporal stasis, for the work would describe those American authors who deserved a place on the mountain.

There are several reasons why Poe decided to abandon a history in favor of a description of the current state of American letters. The first reason may have been a pragmatic one. Poe simply did not have the resources to study early American literature. A decade and a half before, Samuel Kettell's publisher had boasted about investing $1500 in rare books to further Kettell's research. More recently, Rufus Griswold asserted that he had assembled a 700-volume library which he used to compile his *Poets and Poetry of America*.[21] Poe did not have the resources to assemble a fine library to facilitate his research, but his lack of resources was only one possible reason he decided to ignore colonial American authors and to treat contemporary writers exclusively. Quite simply, Poe cared little for early American literature *per se*. Kettell's three-volume anthology, now recognized by literary historians as a scholarly landmark, Poe found trivial and insignificant: "The 'specimens' of Kettell were specimens of nothing but the ignorance and ill taste of the compiler. A large proportion of what he gave to the world as American poetry, to the exclusion of much that was really so, was the doggerel composition of individuals unheard of and undreamed of, except by Mr. Kettell himself."[22] Elsewhere, Poe admitted: "We cannot stand being told . . . that 'Barlow's "Columbiad" is a poem of considerable merit.' "[23] Poe felt comfortable restricting his study to American writers from the first half of the nineteenth century, for he did not see American literature as beginning much before the time of Charles Brockden Brown.

Poe approached Wiley and Putnam editor Evert Duyckinck with his idea for *American Parnassus*. Duyckinck liked it and gave Poe the go-ahead. New responsibilities, however, would soon interfere. In 1845, Poe took the opportunity to become, successively, a contributor to, an editor of, and the proprietor of the *Broadway Journal*. Each role took time away from *American Parnassus*, yet Poe still hoped to complete the book before long. Early on, Poe contributed an essay to the *Broadway Journal* on Nathaniel P. Willis labelled as part of a series, "American Prose Writers." The essay is a spin-off of Poe's ongoing study of American literature, but if it is any indication of the state of *American Parnassus* then the book was still a long way from completion. Instead of treating Willis's life and works, the article provides an extended comparison between fancy and imagination. The comparison is a good one, yet it is out of proportion with Poe's ostensible subject, Nathaniel P. Willis as a prose writer. No further articles appeared in the "American Prose Writers" series, and the demands created by the *Broadway Journal* distracted Poe from completing *American Parnassus*. A surviving letter to Duyckinck from mid-1845 suggests that Poe was still serious about the project and planned to finish it as quickly as possible, yet the letter may have been a mere ploy to eke more money from Wiley and Putnam.[24]

LIVING LITERATI OF THE US

The *Broadway Journal* folded with the 3 January 1846 issue. Relieved from the burden of editing and managing the weekly magazine while sorely needing a steady source of income, Poe tried getting work as a New York correspondent for a London paper and solicited Charles Dickens's help to that end.[25] Seen in isolation, Poe's request to Dickens seems little more than a desperate plea for help, yet understood in light of Poe's conviction that Dickens wrote the *Foreign Quarterly* article, Poe's letter appears to be a genuine effort to describe literary conditions in America for British readers. Dickens was unable to obtain a position for Poe as a correspondent. Poe again placed hope in his book-length study of American literature. He changed titles, too. *American Parnassus* was out. He wrote to Philip Pendleton Cooke, telling him about the book he was planning which would be called " 'The Living Literati of the US.' – or something similar." Poe's letter to Cooke provides the clearest indication of what the work would become, for Poe said that it would contain "personal descriptions, as well as frank opinions of literary merit."[26] The title change confirms that he had abandoned the idea of writing a history and intended to focus on living writers.

"THE LITERATI OF NEW YORK CITY"

When Poe outlined the *Living Literati of the US* to Philip Pendleton Cooke, he let him know that the work would be partially published as a series of magazine articles, "The Literati of New York City." The first installment appeared in *Godey's Lady's Book* for May 1846 with the subtitle, "Some Honest Opinions at Random Respecting Their Autorial Merits, with Occasional Words of Personality." In his prefatory remarks, Poe distinguished between opinion expressed within private literary circles and public opinion, as expressed in the

press. Equating the view of the press with public opinion was a
mistake, Poe thought. Literary opinions in the newspapers and
magazines often get there through the author's agency. Opinions
expressed orally within private literary circles, on the other hand,
more accurately represent the true worth of any given author.
Explaining the purpose of the "Literati" series, Poe wrote,

In the series of papers which I now propose, my design is, in giving my own
unbiased opinion of the *literati* (male and female) of New York, to give at the
same time, very closely if not with absolute accuracy, that of conversational
society in literary circles. It must be expected, of course, that, in
innumerable particulars, I shall differ from the voice, that is to say, from
what appears to be the voice of the public – but this is a matter of no
consequence whatever.[27]

Poe's "Autography" articles had blended private and public by
combining manuscript with print. In the "Literati" Poe combines
private and public by attempting to use a publication to convey
opinions which normally were conveyed orally within private literary
circles.

   After the first installment appeared, one New York paper found
that Poe's "Literati" was "a piece of gratuitous and unpardonable
impertinence" consisting of "ungentlemanly and unpardonable
personalities, and intrusion into the private matters of living men."[28]
Though these remarks were intended as criticism, Poe could not
help but be pleased with them for they showed that he had
accomplished his purpose successfully – that is, he had used a public
forum to voice private opinions.

THE LIVING WRITERS OF AMERICA

After "The Literati of New York City" had run its course, Poe wrote
to George Eveleth, "The unexpected circulation of the series, also,
suggested to me that I might make a hit and some profit, as well as
proper fame, by extending the plan into that of *a book* on American
Letters generally, and keeping the publication in my own hands. I
am now *at* this – body and soul."[29] While his comments to Eveleth
suggest that the periodical series gave him the idea for the book, it
would be more precise to say that the popularity of the periodical
series confirmed the value of a work he had already conceived and
let him know that a similarly written book might prove to be a
commercial success.

Even before the periodical series had finished running, however, the Philadelphia *Saturday Courier* was reporting that Poe intended to continue his sketches "to embrace the whole Union, and the whole to be issued in book form, simultaneously here and in England."[30] The report clearly was planted by Poe, for the emphasis on the publication in England echoes Poe's private comments about the work and verifies his desire to inform British readers about the American literary scene.

Poe's surviving notes for *The Living Writers of America* confirm that the success of the "Literati of New York City" encouraged him to continue a similar book-length work, though he would discard the "petty animosities" which had been a part of the periodical series. Furthermore, the book would allow him to alter the New England bias toward American literature in order to devote more attention to "Southern and Western talent, which upon the whole is greater, more vivid, fresher, than that of the North, less conventional, less conservative." The new approach reinforced Poe's emphasis on a foreign readership. He would take on a role as guide, mapping out the literary territory to those unfamiliar with it. He hoped to correct the stereotypes about American literature, the "English cant about our 'vast forests' etc. Our men of letters generally live in cities, and all great works have thence emanated. Besides the true poet is less affected by the absolute contemplation than the imagination of a great landscape. Living among such scenery is the surest way not to feel it." Poe also emphasized his cosmopolitan approach to litera-ture: "[T]here should be *no* nationality – the world [is] the proper stage."[31]

LITERARY AMERICA

As he planned his book-length work, Poe wrote around the country for details he could use. He wrote to Boston publisher William D. Ticknor for information on one of his authors, Oliver Wendell Holmes: "I am engaged on a work which I will probably call 'Literary America,' and in which I propose to make a general and yet a minute Survey of our Letters."[32] The letter to Ticknor shows that Poe had changed titles again. The new title, *Literary America*, suggests that Poe imagined a geographical organization. *Literary America* would largely consist of biographical sketches similar to those in the "Literati of New York City" series, yet its organizational scheme would be geographical, and the work would contain sections devoted to Boston, Philadelphia, and other major areas of the country. Poe wrote to Virginia author Philip Pendleton Cooke: "Do not forget to send me a few personal details of yourself – such as I give in 'The N. Y. Literati.'"[33] The title change further allowed him to include other critical material besides biography. As he explained his approach to George Eveleth, he wrote, "I intend to be thorough – as far as I can – to examine analytically, without reference to previous opinions by *anybody* – all the salient points of Literature in general – e.g Poetry, The Drama, Criticism, Historical Writing – Versification etc. etc." Poe then directed Eveleth to his forthcoming essay on Hawthorne and his treatise, "The Rationale of Verse."[34] These comments, written late in 1846, suggest that over the course of the year, Poe's conception of the work had undergone another change of direction. It now went beyond literary gossip and critical discussions of individual authors to include some literary theory.

In the same letter, Eveleth also asked about the *Stylus*. Poe affirmed his commitment to the planned magazine, yet asserted that he was biding his time: "But I cannot afford to risk anything by precipitancy – and I *can* afford to wait – at least until I finish *the book*. When that is out, I will start the Mag."[35] A year or so later, he wrote to Eveleth again, letting him know he was hard at work on both the magazine and the book. A new prospectus for the *Stylus* printed in January 1848 confirms that Poe was working on both and suggests that he intended to include sections of *Literary America* in the magazine, which would "include every person of literary note in America; and will investigate carefully, and with rigorous impartiality, the individual claims of each."

Poe's decision to make *Literary America* a part of the *Stylus* reveals that by January 1848 the magazine had taken priority over the book. He quickly regretted having subsumed one project within the other, however. The following month, Poe revised his prospectus for the *Stylus* and omitted the paragraph announcing the serialization of his *Literary America*.

Separate evidence confirms that Poe had decided to make *Literary America* a distinct work in 1848 and that he had begun to prepare a proofsetter's copy. A manuscript fragment containing three of his sketches for the work survives at the Huntington Library. The manuscript begins with a title page neatly printed in Poe's hand, giving the complete title for the work: *Literary America: Some Honest*

Opinions about our Autorial Merits and Demerits with Occasional Words of Personality. The handwritten title page is also dated 1848. Poe even made a half-title page. Clearly, he anticipated that he would have the work completely written, set in type, and published by the year's end. At the time of his death the following year, however, it would remain incomplete.

Conclusion

Literature is the most noble of professions. In fact, it is about the only one fit for a man.
– Poe to Frederick W. Thomas, 14 February 1849

Significant changes in print culture took place during Edgar Allan Poe's lifetime, and he witnessed or participated in most of them. From his boyhood reading to the ambitious projects he left unfinished at the time of his death, Poe confronted innovative technology in book manufacture and changing attitudes toward print. The two are inseparable. Technological developments changed the book's physical appearance, first giving it a mass-produced appearance with the muslin bindings and later, with the pamphlet novel format, making books cheap, throwaway objects. The changes to the book's physical appearance took some getting used to. Books became something everyone could afford, but not without the sacrifice of their elegance. Though the physical changes affected many people's attitudes toward the consumption of books, for Poe, who made literature his profession, the changes had a more profound effect, for they influenced the literature he created.

When Poe was a schoolboy in Great Britain and, later, in Virginia, books opened his mind to the world of the imagination, a world he precociously wished to join. During his adolescence, he expressed a desire to publish his youthful poetic compositions, but his teacher, Joseph Clarke, dissuaded him and, in so doing, taught Poe a valuable lesson about the propriety and impropriety of print. Not all writing, Poe learned, belonged in print. At the University of Virginia he had the chance to exchange ideas about literature among his fellow students, who, for the most part, were the offspring of Virginia gentry. Their literary world scarcely differed from that of their fathers and grandfathers, however. To them, books were important for understanding the ideas of others, but for matters of written self-expression, manuscript sufficed. Though the well-rounded Virginia gentry owned fine libraries, many were content to copy their own compositions by hand and circulate them among a close circle of friends. Poe's life bridged the manuscript culture of the gentlemanly virtuoso and the print culture of the literary professional. When Poe called literature "the most noble of professions" in the year of his death, he made a statement which would have been alien to the previous generation who, at best, might have called *belles lettres* the most noble avocation.

While newspapers and magazines proliferated during the early decades of the nineteenth century, authors and editors remained amateurs. Belletristic contributions to the periodical press were the products of dilettantes. Editors, too, had other professions and sources of income. To repeat a phrase both John Neal and Lambert Wilmer used, men became editors in the early nineteenth century to "work for nothing and find themselves." Though the newspapers and magazines offered writers the opportunity to see their work into print, young Poe was wary of the periodicals. His earliest publications – three separately published collections of poetry – reveal the importance he attached to the book format. As a young adult, Poe saw periodical contributions as ephemeral and books as lasting. His early attitude almost sounds proverbial: magazines are short; books are long.

After publishing his first three books of verse, Poe, partially encouraged by cash prizes the magazines offered, took to story-writing. Though he submitted several short stories to the periodical contests, he continued to uphold the importance of the separately published book to an author's lasting reputation and assembled his short stories as a part of a book-length story cycle, the "Tales of the Folio Club." His attempts to publish the collection were thwarted, however. First Henry Carey and then the Harpers told Poe that collections of stories held little commercial value. The advice of both publishers taught the disappointing lesson that the way to lasting fame and the way to commercial success were two different paths.

The more fiction Poe wrote the more he refined his aesthetic vision and the more ambiguous his attitude toward the book became. He came to believe that the short story, rather than the novel, provided the best vehicle for prose fiction, yet he still considered it important for serious authors to publish books. After he became affiliated with the *Southern Literary Messenger,* however, Poe recognized the literary opportunities a high-quality magazine offered, and he published much fiction and verse within its pages. Simultaneously, he continued seeking a publisher for the "Tales of the Folio Club." Shortly before leaving the *Messenger* he began a book-length story which would become the *Narrative of Arthur Gordon Pym.* In early 1837, the Harpers accepted the book with plans to publish it soon, but the depression that year forced them to withhold the work from publication until the following year. Seeing the Harpers publish Stephens's non-fiction travel narrative, *Incidents of Travel in Egypt, Arabia Petraea, and the Holy Land,* before his own fictional one, Poe learned about the literary priorities of publishers and, presumably, the reading public. Writers of non-fiction continued to hold much more respect in the public's eye than did writers of fanciful stories. The realization may have motivated Poe's desire to write a serious non-fiction work, a book-length history of American literature.

Unable to find any editorial work, Poe considered abandoning the literary profession. The eventual appearance of the *Narrative of Arthur Gordon Pym* did little to help him and his family financially, yet it may have encouraged Poe to continue seeking work in the world of literature. He then found an editorial position with *Burton's Gentleman's Magazine.* Shortly after he became affiliated with *Burton's,* he approached Lea and Blanchard about publishing his collected tales. His behavior clearly indicates that he still believed that an author's lasting reputation rested on the books he published. The belief was strong enough for Poe to be willing to make sacrifices, that is, to forgo royalties, for the sake of gathering his magazine tales between the covers of a book. Lea and Blanchard accepted Poe's sacrifice and agreed to publish the collected tales, and they appeared in the two-volume *Tales of the Grotesque and Arabesque* in late 1839.

The collection of tales, as Henry Carey could have predicted, attracted little attention from the press and sold few copies. These facts alone, however, were insufficient to sour Poe's attitude toward the book format, for much the same could be said about his three volumes of poetry and the *Narrative of Arthur Gordon Pym.* They too had attracted relatively little attention and had sold few copies yet had not changed Poe's belief concerning the importance of book publication for an author. Another factor significantly changed Poe's attitude toward the book format, however. The year the *Tales of the*

Grotesque and Arabesque appeared, pamphlet novels began being published. The importance of the pamphlet novel to Poe's literary career cannot be underestimated. The new format forced Poe to question the value of separately published books. If readers could purchase British and French novels for pennies a copy, then why should they spend a dollar for an American book? For that matter, why should American authors bother writing books their countrymen would not buy?

Poe's disgust with the pamphlet novel coincided with his growing uncertainty about the aesthetic value of the book-length narrative. As the pamphlet novel gained prominence, Poe was attempting his second book-length fictional work, the *Journal of Julius Rodman*. Poe's inability to complete the long story and his more effective reuse of some of *Rodman*'s predominant motifs in "A Descent into the Maelström" confirmed the aesthetic importance of the short tale over the extended narrative. Taken together, the aesthetic failure of *Rodman* and the success of "A Descent into the Maelström" validated the short story as a literary genre over the extended narrative.

The single biggest shift in Poe's attitude toward print culture during his literary career concerns his attitude toward the book as a distinct format. Early on, Poe eschewed periodical publication, which others, including his own brother Henry Poe, took advantage of, but Poe eventually came to champion the periodical. To him, the magazine, not the book, became the vehicle for serious, important literature, and he devoted much of the last decade of his life to imagining, planning, and trying to locate financial support for a magazine of his own and to writing short prose and verse which embodied his magazine aesthetic. He would die in the effort.

Notes

I THE STUDENT AND THE BOOK

1 John Allan to Charles Ellis, 30 October 1815, excerpted in *Log*, 26.
2 Kevin J. Hayes, "Poe's Earliest Reading," *English Language Notes* 32 (March 1995): 39–40.
3 Poe referred to both in his review of Frederick Marryat's *Joseph Rushbrook: Essays and Reviews*, 326.
4 *Log*, 442.
5 *Collected Works* (Mabbott), III: 1130.
6 Thomas Love Peacock, *The Poems of Thomas Love Peacock*, ed. Brimley Johnson (London: George Routledge and Sons, n.d.), 200.
7 Review of James Pedder, *Frank, Burton's Gentleman's Magazine* 6 (May 1840): 250.
8 *Log*, 279.
9 "Emilia Harrington," *SLM* 2 (February 1836): 191.
10 "Daniel Defoe," *Essays and Reviews*, 201.
11 "Theodore S. Fay," *Essays and Reviews*, 547.
12 *SLM* 2 (October 1836): 669.
13 Review of Hugh A. Pue, *Grammar of the English Language, Graham's Magazine* 19 (July 1841): 45.
14 "Fifty Suggestions," *Brevities*, 498.
15 Hayes, "Poe's Earliest Reading," 41.
16 "Armstrong's Notices," *SLM* 2 (June 1836): 450.
17 *Collected Works* (Mabbott), II: 430.
18 Quoted in Mary Newton Stanard, *Edgar Allan Poe Letters Till Now Unpublished in the Valentine Museum, Richmond, Virginia* (1925; reprinted, New York: Haskell House, 1973), 17. For a survey of Poe's Latin quotations and references, see Emma Katherine Norman, "Poe's Knowledge of Latin," *American Literature* 6 (March 1934): 72–77. See also T. O. Mabbott, "Evidence that Poe Knew Greek," *Notes and Queries* 185 (17 July 1943): 39–40.
19 In the notes to his edition of Poe's *Politan: An Unfinished Tragedy* (Menasha, WI: Collegiate Press, 1923), Thomas Ollive Mabbott mentions a copy of *Aesopi Fabulae* with evidence of Poe's ownership in the

collection of J. H. Whitty. Mabbott mentioned the volume again in "A List of Books from Poe's Library," *Notes and Queries* 200 (1955): 222, but was unaware of its whereabouts at the time.

20 William Elijah Hunter, "Poe and His English Schoolmaster," *Athenaeum* 2660 (19 October 1878): 496. See also, Lewis Chase, "John Bransby, Poe's Schoolmaster," *Athenaeum*, 4605 (May 1916): 221–222.

21 Hayes, "Poe's Earliest Reading," 42.

22 John Allan to William Galt, 28 September 1819; Allan to Galt, 27 November 1819; Allan to Galt, 20 January 1820; *Log*, 42–43.

23 *Log*, 47.

24 *Log*, 51.

25 Review of Charles Anthon, ed., *Select Orations of Cicero: with an English Commentary and Historical, Geographical and Legal Indexes*, *SLM* 3 (January 1837): 72.

26 Herbert Marshall McLuhan, "Edgar Poe's Tradition," *Sewanee Review* 52 (January 1944): 24–33.

27 *Log*, 53.

28 Poe to Nathan C. Brooks, 4 September 1838, *Letters*, I: 112.

29 Poe to Beverley Tucker, 1 December 1835, *Letters*, I: 78.

30 *Log*, 58.

31 Poe to John Allan, 3 January 1831, *Letters*, I: 40; Poe to Allan, 25 May 1826, *Letters*, I: 4–5.

32 Ruth Leigh Hudson, "Poe and Disraeli," *American Literature* 8 (January 1937): 402–404.

33 *Log*, 71.

34 George Bernard Shaw, "Edgar Allan Poe," *Nation* 4 (16 January 1909): 602.

35 For the best discussion of plantation libraries in early nineteenth-century Virginia, see Richard Beale Davis, *Intellectual Life in Jefferson's Virginia, 1790–1830* (1964; reprinted, Knoxville: University of Tennessee Press, 1972), 73–188.

36 Kevin J. Hayes, *Folklore and Book Culture* (Knoxville: University of Tennessee Press, 1997), 89–98.

37 Philip Alexander Bruce, *History of the University of Virginia, 1819–1919* (New York: Macmillan, 1920–1922), II: 185–186.

38 *Log*, 75.

39 *Log*, 69–70.

40 *Dictionary of National Biography*, ed. Leslie Stephen and Sidney Lee, 22 vols. (Oxford: Oxford University Press 1885–1901), XI: 1199–1202; A. W. Ward and A. R. Waller, *The Cambridge History of English Literature* (New York: G. P. Putnam's Sons, 1917), 14: 58–61.

41 "Variety," *Port Folio* new ser. 1 (25 January 1806): 44–45.

42 "Hume and Robertson Compared," *Port Folio*, ser. 3, vol. 4 (October 1810): 330.

43 Kenneth Walter Cameron, "Notes on Young Poe's Reading," *American Transcendental Quarterly* 24 (Fall 1974): 33–34; *Log*, 72.
44 *Log*, 69.
45 Floyd Stovall, "Edgar Poe and the University of Virginia," *Virginia Quarterly Review* 43 (Spring 1967): 301.
46 Bruce, *History of the University of Virginia*, II: 84.
47 "Variety," 44.
48 Poe to John Allan, 21 September 1826, *Letters*, I: 6.
49 Poe to John Allan, 21 September 1826, *Letters*, I: 6; Harry Clemons, *The University of Virginia Library, 1825–1950: Story of a Jeffersonian Foundation* (Charlottesville: University of Virginia Library, 1954), 12.
50 Cameron, "Notes on Young Poe's Reading," 33; *Log*, 73.
51 E. Millicent Sowerby, *Catalogue of the Library of Thomas Jefferson* (1952–1959; reprinted, Charlottesville: University Press of Virginia, 1983), no. 4819.
52 Poe to Frederick W. Thomas, 26 November 1841, *Letters*, I: 190.
53 Poe mentioned Fénelon's work in both of his reviews of Lydia Maria Child's *Philothea: A Romance*; *SLM* 2 (September 1836): 659–662, and *Broadway Journal* 1 (24 May 1845): 342–345. For a discussion of the work's popularity in early America, see Kevin J. Hayes, *A Colonial Woman's Bookshelf* (Knoxville: University of Tennessee Press, 1996), 62.
54 Agnes M. Bondurant, *Poe's Richmond* (Richmond: Garrett and Massie, 1942), 87.
55 Poe to Frederick W. Thomas, 3 February 1842, *Letters*, I: 192.
56 "Paul Ulric," *SLM* 2 (February 1836): 177.
57 *Log*, 73.
58 "Professor Dew's Address," *SLM* 2 (October 1836): 721.
59 Padraic Colum, Introduction, *Edgar Allan Poe's Tales of Mystery and Imagination* (London: J. M. Dent, 1916), xiii.
60 *Log*, 78.
61 Review of Alessandro Manzoni, *I Promessi Sposi*, trans. G. W. Featherstonhaugh, *SLM* 1 (May 1835): 522.
62 "Gil Blas and Don Quixote," *Athenaeum* [Boston] 8 (1 November 1820): 123.
63 "Francis Lieber," *Essays and Reviews*, 664.
64 "Nuts to Crack," *SLM* 2 (December 1835): 49. The quotation which ends this chapter comes from a letter from Poe to John Allan, 19 March 1827, *Letters*, I: 7.

2 POETRY IN MANUSCRIPT AND PRINT

1 "Editorial Miscellanies," *Essays and Reviews*, 1086.
2 Poe to John Allan, 25 May 1826, *Letters*, I: 5.
3 Review of *The Raven and Other Poems*, *Anglo-American* 6 (22 November 1845): 116.

4 *Log,* 47.

5 I. B. Cauthen, Jr., "Poe's *Alone*: Its Background, Source, and Manuscript," *Studies in Bibliography* 3 (1950–1951): 287.

6 Herman Melville, *Pierre: Or, The Ambiguities,* ed. Harrison Hayford, Hershel Parker, and G. Thomas Tanselle (Evanston and Chicago: Northwestern University Press and The Newberry Library, 1971), 251.

7 For a good selection of nineteenth-century album verse, see Vance Randolph and May Kennedy McCord, "Autograph Albums in the Ozarks," *Journal of American Folklore* 61 (1948): 182–193, and Alan Dundes, "Some Examples of Infrequently Reported Autograph Verse," *Southern Folklore Quarterly* 26 (June 1962): 127–130. Dundes includes a detailed bibliography of other collections of autograph verse.

8 *Collected Works* (Mabbott), 1: 15.

9 Charles Francis Potter, "Round Went the Album," *New York Folklore Quarterly* 4 (Spring 1948): 7. Dundes, "Some Examples," 130, records another nineteenth-century instance of this traditional verse.

10 Cauthen, "Poe's *Alone*," 291.

11 Donald H. Reiman, *The Study of Modern Manuscripts: Public, Confidential, and Private* (Baltimore: Johns Hopkins University Press, 1993).

12 "Pinakidia" and "Marginalia," *Brevities,* 11, 176.

13 William Wirt to Poe, 11 May 1829, excerpted in *Log,* 92.

14 John Neal, *Wandering Recollections of a Somewhat Busy Life: An Autobiography* (Boston: Roberts Brothers, 1869), 162.

15 Poe to John Allan, 20 May 1829, *Letters,* 1: 17.

16 Poe to John Allan, 29 May 1829, *Letters,* 1: 21.

17 Poe to Isaac Lea, before 27 May 1829, *Letters,* 1: 18; *Collected Works* (Mabbott), 1: 147.

18 *Log,* 109.

19 *Log,* 108.

20 *Collected Works* (Mabbott), 1: 151.

21 *Log,* 117.

22 *Log,* 118.

23 John E. Semmes, *John H. B. Latrobe and His Times, 1803–1891* (Baltimore: Norman, Remington, 1917), 559–560.

24 Charles Baudelaire, *Baudelaire on Poe,* trans. and ed. Lois Hylsop and Francis E. Hylsop, Jr. (State College, PA: Bald Eagle Press, 1952), 125.

25 "Marginalia," *Brevities,* 108.

3 BALTIMORE BOOK CULTURE

1 Poe to John Allan, 10 August 1829, *Letters,* 1: 30; John Hill Hewitt, *Shadows on the Wall: Or, Glimpses of the Past* (1877; reprinted, New York: AMS Press, 1971), 88. Hewitt's comments are partially reprinted in David K. Jackson, "A Man Named Bool: A Shadow on the Wall," *Poe Studies* 10 (December 1977): 44.

2 Rollo G. Silver, "The Baltimore Book Trade, 1800–1825," *Bulletin of the New York Public Library* 57 (1953): 184.

3 Hewitt, *Shadows on the Wall*, 90, 88.

4 John Tebbel, *A History of Book Publishing in the United States* (New York: R. R. Bowker, 1972–1981), 1: 220.

5 Hervey Allen, *Israfel: The Life and Times of Edgar Allan Poe* (New York: Farrar and Rinehart, 1934), 267.

6 John E. Semmes, *John H. B. Latrobe and His Times, 1803–1891* (Baltimore: Norman, Remington, 1917), 105.

7 David Kaser, *A Book for a Sixpence: The Circulating Library in America* (Pittsburgh: Beta Phi Mu, 1980), 77–78. Poe refers to Robinson in a letter to Joseph Evans Snodgrass, 20 January 1840, *Letters*, 1: 127.

8 Poe would satirize Franklin's *Autobiography* in "The Business Man." See J. A. Leo Lemay, "Poe's 'The Business Man': Its Contexts and Satire of Franklin's *Autobiography*," *Poe Studies* 15 (December 1982): 29–37.

9 Benjamin Franklin, *Benjamin Franklin's Autobiography: A Norton Critical Edition*, ed. J. A. Leo Lemay and P. M. Zall (New York: Norton, 1986), 57.

10 Stuart C. Sherman, "The Library Company of Baltimore, 1795–1854," *Maryland Historical Magazine* 39 (March 1944): 21.

11 Library Company of Baltimore, *A Catalogue of the Books* (Baltimore: Prentiss and Cole, 1802); Library Company of Baltimore, *A Supplement to the Catalogue of Books* (Baltimore: J. Robinson, 1816). Poe's opinion of Byron's *English Bards and Scotch Reviewers* occurs in his review of Robert Folkestone Williams's *Mephistopheles in England, Or The Confessions of a Prime Minister*, *SLM* 1 (September 1835): 776.

12 Hewitt, *Shadows on the Wall*, 48; *Log*, xviii.

13 Poe to William H. Carpenter, J. S. Norris, and James Brown, 28 February 1837, *Letters*, 1: 111; *BAL*, no. 16129.

14 Review of Frederick Marryat, *The Phantom Ship*, *Burton's Gentleman's Magazine* 4 (June 1839): 358–359.

15 Review of William Beckford, *Recollections of an Excursion to the Monasteries of Alcobaca and Batalha*, *SLM* 1 (August 1835): 714.

16 "William Gilmore Simms," *Essays and Reviews*, 891.

17 Poe's comments occur in his review of Seba Smith's later work, *Powhatan; A Metrical Romance, in Seven Cantos*, *Essays and Reviews*, 918. ORBIS, the Yale University online library catalog, states that the Beinecke copy of Smith's *Powhatan* was formerly in Poe's possession, but neither copy in the Beinecke Library contains evidence of Poe's ownership nor do external documents survive to verify Poe's ownership (Ellen R. Cordes to Kevin J. Hayes, 25 November 1996).

18 Edwin Wolf, II, "Horace Wemyss Smith's Recollections of Poe," *Library Chronicle of the University of Pennsylvania* 17 (Summer 1951): 93.

19 Review of Frances Trollope, *Paris and the Parisians in 1835*, *SLM* 2 (May 1836): 394.

20 Review of *North American Review* (51 [October 1835]), *SLM* 2 (December 1835): 64.
21 Hewitt, *Shadows on the Wall*, 16; Semmes, *John H. B. Latrobe*, 102.
22 John Neal, *Wandering Recollections of a Somewhat Busy Life: An Autobiography* (Boston: Roberts Brothers, 1869), 175; Hewitt, *Shadows on the Wall*, 16.
23 Neal, *Wandering Recollections*, 210.
24 John P. Kennedy, quoted in John Earle Uhler, "The Delphian Club: A Contribution to the Literary History of Baltimore in the Early Nineteenth Century," *Maryland Historical Magazine* 20 (December 1925): 311.
25 Uhler, "Delphian Club," 327.
26 Semmes, *John H. B. Latrobe*, 561.
27 Latrobe recalled, "Mr. Gwynn saw that I was working hard to become a lawyer and suggested that I should begin to write a book on the duties of a Justice of the Peace and Constable, by way of learning something of these subjects myself"; quoted in Semmes, *John H. B. Latrobe*, 102. Neal's experience with Gwynn was almost identical. When he was unable to find a book on the subject he was studying, he asked Gwynn what to do. Gwynn responded, "Write a book on the subject!"; *Wandering Recollections*, 113.
28 Poe to William Gwynn, 6 May 1831, *Letters*, 1: 45.
29 Semmes, *John H. B. Latrobe*, 561.
30 Neal, *Wandering Recollections*, 162–163.
31 Hewitt, *Shadows on the Wall*, 89.
32 *Log*, 103.
33 Lambert A. Wilmer, *Our Press Gang; or, A Complete Exposition of the Corruptions and Crimes of the American Newspapers* (Philadelphia: J. T. Lloyd, 1859), 24.
34 Lambert A. Wilmer, "Recollections of Edgar A. Poe," in Lambert A. Wilmer, *Merlin: Baltimore, 1827*, ed. Thomas Ollive Mabbott (New York: Scholars' Facsimiles and Reprints, 1941), 30.
35 "Emilia Harrington," *SLM* 2 (February 1836): 192.
36 Wilmer, *Our Press Gang*, 25.
37 Review of Delia S. Bacon, *The Bride of Fort Edward*, *Burton's Gentleman's Magazine* 5 (September 1839): 169.
38 Review of John Pendleton Kennedy, *Horse Shoe Robinson: A Tale of the Tory Ascendancy*, *SLM* 1 (May 1835): 522.
39 James Southall Wilson, "The Devil Was in It," *American Mercury* 24 (October 1931): 216. For more on the "Folio Club" tales, see Richard P. Benton, "The Tales: 1831–1835," in *A Companion to Poe Studies*, ed. Eric W. Carlson (Westport, CT: Greenwood Press, 1996), 110–113; Benjamin Franklin Fisher, IV, *The Very Spirit of Cordiality: The Literary Uses of Alcohol and Alcoholism in the Tales of Edgar Allan Poe* (Baltimore: Enoch Pratt Free Library and the Edgar Allan Poe Society, 1978); and G. R. Thompson, *Poe's Fiction: Romantic Irony in the Gothic Tales* (Madison: University of Wisconsin Press, 1973), 39–42.

40 John Neal, *Randolph, A Novel* (n.p.: n.p., 1823), I: 316–317.
41 *Collected Works* (Mabbott), II: 205.
42 Quoted in Semmes, *John H. B. Latrobe*, 372. Hewitt's description of Gwynn is more euphemistic: "He might have been classed with portly men, though he was not over-tall" (*Shadows on the Wall*, 16).
43 *Collected Works* (Mabbott), II: 204.
44 Semmes, *John H. B. Latrobe*, 559.
45 *Log*, 134.
46 Poe to Joseph Evans Snodgrass, 4 June 1842, *Letters*, I: 201.
47 John H. B. Latrobe to Charles Chauncey Burr, 7 December 1852, excerpted in *Log*, 132.
48 In his "Literati" sketch of Richard Adams Locke, Poe misremembered the publisher of the 1834 edition of Herschel's *Treatise on Astronomy*, for Carey, Lea, and Blanchard published it, not the Harpers; *Essays and Reviews*, 1215.
49 John H. B. Latrobe to Charles Chauncey Burr, 7 December 1852, excerpted in *Log*, 132.
50 Lambert A. Wilmer, *The Quacks of Helicon* (Philadelphia: J. W. Macclefield, 1841), lines 973–976.
51 Henry C. Carey to John P. Kennedy, 26 November 1834, as excerpted in *Log*, 142.
52 Review of *The Gift*, *SLM* 1 (September 1835): 780.
53 Henry C. Carey to John P. Kennedy, 26 November 1834, as excerpted in *Log*, 142.
54 John P. Kennedy to Poe, 22 December 1834, *Complete Works* (Harrison), XVII: 3.
55 *Log*, 149.
56 David K. Jackson, "Four of Poe's Critiques in the Baltimore Newspapers," *Modern Language Notes* 50 (April 1935): 255.
57 Jackson, "Four of Poe's Critiques," 256.

4 BOOKSELLERS' BANQUET

1 William Gowans, *Catalogue 28* (1870), 11, as quoted in Roger E. Stoddard, *"Put a Resolute Hart to a Steep Hill": William Gowans, Antiquary and Bookseller* (New York: Book Arts Press of the School of Library Service, Columbia University, 1990), 26.
2 *Broadway Journal* 2 (20 September 1845): 168.
3 "Recollections of Coleridge," *SLM* 2 (June 1836): 453; Stoddard, *"Put a Resolute Hart"*, 35.
4 Mabbott, *Collected Works*, II: 419, suggests that Poe may have learned about some of the rare books mentioned in "The Fall of the House of Usher" from Gowans.
5 "Bookseller's Dinner," *Morning Courier and New-York Enquirer*, 1 April 1837.

6 "Joseph Rodman Drake – Fitz-Greene Halleck," *Essays and Reviews*, 512.

7 "Rufus W. Griswold," *Essays and Reviews*, 551; Poe to John Keese, 26 May 1845, *Letters*, I: 289; Poe to Evert A. Duyckinck, 28 April 1846, *Letters*, II: 316.

8 Philip Hone, *The Diary of Philip Hone*, ed. Bayard Tuckerman (New York: Dodd, Mead, 1889), I: 249–250.

9 James Grant Wilson, *The Memorial History of the City of New-York from Its First Settlement to the Year 1892* (New York: New-York History Company, 1893), III: 369.

10 "The Bookseller's Festival," [New York] *Evening Post*, 3 April 1837. Much of the following information is taken from this lengthy account and will not be documented separately.

11 Hone, *Diary*, I: 250.

12 John Tebbel, *A History of Book Publishing in the United States* (New York: R. R. Bowker, 1972–1981), I: 225–227.

13 "Prospectus of the Penn Magazine," *Essays and Reviews*, 1024.

14 "Supplement to the Southern Literary Messenger," *SLM* 2 (January 1836): 133–134.

15 "Marginalia," *Brevities*, 339.

16 *Collected Works* (Mabbott), III: 1141.

17 [James Gordon Bennett,] "Great Literary Festival," [New York] *Herald*, 4 April 1837.

18 "The Booksellers' Festival," *New-York Daily Express*, 4 April 1837.

19 "William Leete Stone," *Essays and Reviews*, 950.

20 *Log*, 198.

21 "Joseph Rodman Drake – Fitz-Greene Halleck," *Essays and Reviews*, 530.

22 "The Literati of New York City," *Essays and Reviews*, 1159.

23 "William Cullen Bryant," *Essays and Reviews*, 441–442.

24 Frederick W. Thomas to Poe, 3 August 1841, *Complete Works* (Harrison), XVII: 97.

25 "Erato," *SLM* 2 (July 1836): 513.

26 Review of Charles Fenno Hoffman, *A Winter in the West*, *SLM* 1 (April 1835): 459.

27 "A Chapter on Autography," *Complete Works* (Harrison), XV: 179.

28 "Critical Notices and Literary Intelligence," *SLM* 1 (August 1835): 715.

29 Hone, *Diary*, I: 249.

30 Review of Washington Irving, *A Tour on the Prairies*, *SLM* 1 (April 1835): 456.

31 Eugene Exman, *The Brothers Harper: A Unique Publishing Partnership and Its Impact upon the Cultural Life of America from 1817 to 1853* (New York: Harper and Row, 1965), 90.

32 "New-York Booksellers' Dinner," *American Monthly Magazine*, new ser. 3 (May 1837): 521.

33 "Public Dinner of the Booksellers and Publishers," *Albion* 5 (1 April 1837): 103.
34 Quoted in Tebbel, *A History of Book Publishing*, 1: 233.
35 [James Gordon Bennett,] "The Committee of the Booksellers," [New York] *Herald*, 13 April 1837.
36 [James Gordon Bennett,] "Literary Taste," [New York] *Herald*, 4 May 1837.
37 "Prospectus of the Stylus," *Essays and Reviews*, 1035.
38 "New-York Booksellers' Dinner," *American Monthly Magazine*, new ser. 3 (May 1837): 524.
39 "Godwin's Necromancy," *SLM* 2 (December 1835): 65.
40 "Booksellers," *New-Yorker* 3 (1 April 1837): 29.

5 THE NOVEL

1 Thomas W. White to Beverley Tucker, 26 April 1837, excerpted in *Log*, 244.
2 Harper and Brothers to Poe, June 1836, quoted in Arthur Hobson Quinn, *Edgar Allan Poe: A Critical Biography* (1941; reprinted, Baltimore: Johns Hopkins University Press, 1998), 251. This letter is also the source for the chapter motto.
3 Review of Robert M. Bird, *Hawks of Hawk-Hollow; A Tradition of Pennsylvania*, *SLM* 2 (December 1835): 45–46.
4 James Kirke Paulding to Poe, 3 March 1836, excerpted in *Log*, 193.
5 Edgar Allan Poe, *The Imaginary Voyages: The Narrative of Arthur Gordon Pym, The Unparalleled Adventure of One Hans Pfaall, The Journal of Julius Rodman*, ed. Burton R. Pollin (Boston: Twayne, 1981), 428.
6 "A Valentine to — — — —" *Edgar Allan Poe: Poetry and Tales*, ed. Patrick F. Quinn (New York: Library of America, 1984), 86.
7 Randel Helm, "Another Source for Poe's *Arthur Gordon Pym*" *American Literature* 41 (January 1970): 572–575; Burton R. Pollin, "Poe and Daniel Defoe: A Significant Relationship," *Topic* 30 (Fall 1976): 19; Poe to Evert Duyckinck, 8 March 1849, *Letters*, II 433.
8 "Daniel Defoe," *Essays and Reviews*, 201.
9 "Emilia Harrington," *SLM* 2 (February 1836): 191.
10 *Log*, 244.
11 Quoted in Isaac Newton Phelps Stokes, *The Iconography of Manhattan Island, 1498–1909*, 6 vols. (New York: Robert H. Dodd, 1915–1928), 1748.
12 Eugene Exman, *The Brothers Harper: A Unique Publishing Partnership and Its Impact upon the Cultural Life of America from 1817 to 1853* (New York: Harper and Row, 1965), 95.
13 "John L. Stephens," *Essays and Reviews*, 941.
14 Poe to James Kirke Paulding, 19 July 1838, *Letters*, II: 681.
15 Review of *The Narrative of Arthur Gordon Pym*, *Metropolitan Magazine* 23 (November 1838): 81.

16 *Log*, 250.
17 *Log*, 254.
18 Review of *The Narrative of Arthur Gordon Pym*, [New York] *Albion*, new ser. 6 (18 August 1838): 263.
19 "Novels of the Month," *Monthly Review* 3 (October 1838): 567.
20 "Narrative of Arthur Gordon Pym, of Nantucket, North America," *Court Gazette and Fashionable Guide* 1 (13 October 1838): 445.
21 Christina Rossetti to William Michael Rossetti, 31 August 1849, *The Letters of Christina Rossetti*, vol. 1: *1843–1873*, ed. Anthony H. Harrison (Charlottesville: University Press of Virginia, 1997), 22.
22 Poe to William E. Burton, 1 June 1840, *Letters*, 1: 130.
23 Evert A. Duyckinck, *Cyclopaedia of American Literature Embracing Personal and Critical Notices of Authors, and Selections from Their Writings* (New York: C. Scribner, 1855), II: 538.
24 James Kirke Paulding to Poe, 17 March 1836, *Complete Works* (Harrison), XVII: 32.
25 "James Fenimore Cooper," *Essays and Reviews*, 479–480.
26 "James Fenimore Cooper," *Essays and Reviews*, 479–480.

6 POE'S LIBRARY

1 Poe to John Allan, 19 March 1827, *Letters*, 1: 8.
2 Poe to John Allan, 28 June 1830, *Letters*, 1: 37.
3 Poe to James R. Lowell, 2 July 1844, *Letters*, 1: 258.
4 Poe to John P. Kennedy, 22 January 1836, *Letters*, 1: 81; Harper and Brothers to Poe, June 1836, quoted in Arthur Hobson Quinn, *Edgar Allan Poe: A Critical Biography* (1941; reprinted, Baltimore: Johns Hopkins University Press, 1998), 251.
5 Poe to Frederick W. Thomas, 21 September 1842, *Letters*, 1: 214.
6 Frederick W. Thomas to Poe, 7 December 1840, *Complete Works* (Harrison), XVII: 65.
7 *BAL*, 1: xxx–xxxiii; Joseph W. Rogers, "The Rise of American Edition Binding," in *Bookbinding in America*, ed. Hellmut Lehmann-Haupt (New York: Bowker, 1967), 135–142.
8 Review of *Sallust's Jugurthine War*, ed. Charles Anthon, *SLM* 2 (May 1836): 392.
9 *BAL*, 1: xxxi; Rogers, "The Rise of American Edition Binding," 148.
10 *BAL*, no. 16128.
11 "William Leete Stone," *Essays and Reviews*, 942.
12 Review of Lydia Maria Child, *Philothea: A Romance*, *SLM* 2 (September 1836): 659.
13 *BAL*, no. 3130.
14 "Augustus Baldwin Longstreet," *Essays and Reviews*, 796.
15 *Writings in The Broadway Journal: Nonfictional Prose*, ed. Burton R. Pollin (New York: Gordian, 1986), 1: 250.

16 "The Southern Literary Messenger," *Broadway Journal* 1 (22 March 1845): 183.

17 Beverley Tucker to Poe, 5 December 1835, *Complete Works* (Harrison), XVII: 24.

18 "Eaton Stannard Barrett," *Essays and Reviews*, 109.

19 Poe to George W. Eveleth, 15 December 1846, *Letters*, II: 333.

20 "Marginalia," *Brevities*, 107–108.

21 "A Chapter of Autography," *Complete Works* (Harrison), XV: 181–182. Charles Anthon to Poe, 2 November 1844, *Complete Works* (Harrison), XVII: 193, wrote, "The MSS., which you were kind enough to send, can be obtained by you at any time on calling at my residence."

22 *Collected Works* (Mabbott), II: 503.

23 W. T. Bandy, "Poe, Duane, and Duffee," *University of Mississippi Studies in English*, new ser. 3 (1982): 81–95.

24 "Editorial Miscellanies," *Essays and Reviews*, 1090.

25 Austin Baxter Keep, *History of the New York Society Library* (1908; reprinted, Boston: Gregg, 1972), 400–401.

26 Keep, *History of the New York Society Library*, 404.

27 Poe to Evert A. Duyckinck, 24 December 1846, *Letters*, II: 334.

28 Poe to Evert A. Duyckinck, 28 April 1846, *Letters*, II: 316.

29 Thomas Mabbott, "A List of Books from Poe's Library," *Notes and Queries* 200 (1955): 222–223; Poe to John Keese, 26 May 1845, *Letters*, I: 289.

30 Killis Campbell, "Poe's Reading: Addenda and Corrigenda," *University of Texas Studies in English* 7 (1927): 175.

31 Poe to John Keese, 26 May 1845, *Letters*, I: 289.

32 Poe to Bayard Taylor, 15 June 1848, *Letters*, II: 371.

33 Poe to Mary Osborne, 15 July 1848, *Letters*, II: 375–376.

34 R. H. Horne to Poe, 17 May 1845, *Complete Works* (Harrison), XVIII: 210.

35 William Gowans, *Catalogue 27* (1869), 30, quoted in Stoddard, *"Put a Resolute Hart"*, 26.

36 William Gowans, *Catalogue 27* (1869), 30, quoted in Stoddard, *"Put a Resolute Hart"*, 26.

37 Merton M. Sealts, Jr., *Melville's Reading: Revised and Enlarged Edition* (Columbia: University of South Carolina Press, 1988), no. 103.

38 Mary Gove Nichols, *Reminiscences of Edgar Allan Poe* (1929; reprinted, New York: Haskall House, 1974), 9.

39 Poe to Marie Louise Shew, May 1847, *Letters*, II: 350.

40 Elizabeth Barrett to Poe, April 1846, *Complete Works* (Harrison), XVII: 229.

41 *Edgar Allan Poe: Poetry and Tales*, ed. Patrick F. Quinn (New York: Library of America, 1984), 225–226.

42 *Collected Works* (Mabbott), III: 1246–1247.

7 CHEAP BOOKS AND EXPENSIVE MAGAZINES

1 Frank Luther Mott, *A History of American Magazines 1741–1850*, vol. 1 (1930; reprinted, Cambridge: The Belknap Press of Harvard University Press, 1966), 360. Hellmut Lehmann-Haupt, Lawrence C. Wroth, and Rollo G. Silver, *The Book in America: A History of the Making and Selling of Books in the United States*, 2nd edn. (New York: R. R. Bowker, 1952), 130; Frank Luther Mott, *Golden Multitudes: The Story of Best Sellers in the United States* (New York: Macmillan, 1947), 77; Frank L. Schick, *The Paperbound Book in America: The History of Paperbacks and Their European Background* (New York: R. R. Bowker, 1958), 48; Raymond Howard Shove, *Cheap Book Production in the United States, 1870–1891* (Urbana: University of Illinois Library, 1937), v–vii.

2 Charles Lyell, *A Second Visit to the United States of North America* (New York: Harper and Brothers, 1849), II: 251, 253.

3 "Editor's Table," *Arthur's Ladies' Magazine* 2 (November 1844): 242.

4 Nathaniel Hawthorne, *The American Notebooks*, ed. Claude M. Simpson (Columbus: Ohio State University Press, 1971), 488.

5 Kevin J. Hayes, "Railway Reading," *Proceedings of the American Antiquarian Society* 106 (1997): 301–305.

6 X.L.O., "The Mission of Novelettes," *Holden's Dollar Monthly* 1 (April 1848): 218.

7 "William Harrison Ainsworth," *Essays and Reviews*, 101.

8 "Some Secrets of the Magazine Prison-House," *Essays and Reviews*, 1036–1038.

9 "The Literati of New York City," *Essays and Reviews*, 1203.

10 Michael Sadleir, *XIX Century Fiction: A Bibliographical Record* (Berkeley: University of California Press, 1951), II: 142–145. For additional information on Cunningham's edition of *Pym*, see T. E. Elwell, "A Poe Story," *TLS* 23 October 1943, 516; and G. B. Dunlop, "A Poe Story," *TLS* 15 January 1944, 36.

11 Philip P. Cooke to Poe, 4 August 1846, *Complete Works* (Harrison), XVII: 263–264.

12 *BAL*, no. 16203.

13 *BAL*, no. 16138.

14 *Log*, 426, 429.

15 *BAL*, no. 8075.

16 Poe to Washington Irving, 21 June 1841, *Letters*, I: 162.

17 Poe to Edward H. N. Patterson, 7 August 1849, *Letters*, II: 457.

18 Poe to Edward H. N. Patterson, 30? April 1849, *Letters*, II: 440.

19 Poe to Thomas W. White, 22 June 1835, *Letters*, I: 64.

20 "Nathaniel Hawthorne," *Essays and Reviews*, 588.

21 ["Exordium,"] *Graham's Magazine* 20 (January 1842): 68.

22 Review of *London Quarterly Review*, *SLM* 1 (April 1835): 458.

23 "William Leete Stone," *Essays and Reviews*, 942.

24 Poe to Joseph Evans Snodgrass, 17 January 1841, *Letters*, I: 152.

25 Poe to J. Sartain, 9 February 1849, in Heidi M. Schultz, "Edgar Allan Poe Submits 'The Bells' to *Sartain's Magazine*," *Resources for American Literary Study* 22 (1996): 169.

26 Poe to Frederick W. Thomas, 25 February 1843, *Letters*, I: 224.

27 *Writings in The* Broadway Journal*: Nonfictional Prose*, ed. Burton R. Pollin (New York: Gordian, 1986), 128.

28 *Prospectus of the Stylus*, in *Essays and Reviews*, 1033.

29 Poe to George W. Eveleth, 15 December 1846, *Letters*, II: 333.

8 THE ROAD TO 'LITERARY AMERICA'

1 "Augustus Baldwin Longstreet," *Essays and Reviews*, 778.

2 Review of B. B. Thatcher, *Traits of the Tea Party*, *SLM* 2 (March 1836): 292.

3 Review of John Quincy Adams, *The Jubilee of the Constitution*, *Burton's Gentleman's Magazine* 5 (August 1839): 114.

4 Review of Benvenuto Cellini, *Memoirs of Benvenuto Cellini*, *Broadway Journal* 2 (1 November 1845): 257.

5 Review of Isaac D'Israeli, *Miscellanies of Literature*, *Graham's Magazine* 19 (July 1841): 47.

6 "The Literati of New York City," *Essays and Reviews*, 1121.

7 Thomas W. White to Poe, 29 September 1835, *Complete Works* (Harrison), XVII: 21.

8 "Autography," *Collected Works* (Mabbott), II: 272.

9 Poe to James R. Lowell, 18 August 1844, *Letters*, I: 261.

10 Poe to Joseph Evans Snodgrass, 4 June 1842, *Letters*, I: 202.

11 *Log*, 447–448.

12 "Editorial Miscellanies," *Essays and Reviews*, 1088.

13 "American Poetry," [London] *Foreign Quarterly Review* 32 (January 1844): 321.

14 "Editorial Miscellanies," *Essays and Reviews*, 1103.

15 James Russell Lowell to Poe, 27 June 1844, *Complete Works* (Harrison), XVII: 181.

16 "The Literati of New York City," *Essays and Reviews*, 1134.

17 Poe to Thomas H. Chivers, 10 July 1844, *Letters*, I: 259.

18 "Literary America," Huntington Library manuscript, no. HM1184.

19 James Russell Lowell to Poe, 27 June 1844, excerpted in *Log*, 465.

20 Huntington Library manuscript, no. HM1184.

21 Kermit Vanderbilt, *American Literature and the Academy: The Roots, Growth, and Maturity of a Profession* (Philadelphia: University of Pennsylvania Press, 1986), 57.

22 "Rufus W. Griswold," *Essays and Reviews*, 550.

23 Review of Roswell Park, *Pantology; or A Systematic Survey of Human Knowledge, Graham's Magazine* 20 (March 1842): 191.

24 Poe to Evert A. Duyckinck, 26 June 1845, *Letters*, I: 290.

25 Charles Dickens to Edgar Allan Poe, 19 March 1846, *The Letters of Charles Dickens: The Pilgrim Edition*, ed. Kathleen Tillotson *et al.*, vol. IV (Oxford: Clarendon Press, 1977), 523.

26 Poe to Philip P. Cooke, 16 April 1846, *Letters*, II: 314.

27 "The Literati of New York City," *Essays and Reviews*, 1120.

28 *Log*, 636.

29 Poe to George W. Eveleth, 15 December 1846, *Letters*, II: 332.

30 *Log*, 659.

31 Burton R. Pollin, "The Living Writers of America: A Manuscript by Edgar Allan Poe," *Studies in the American Renaissance, 1991*, ed. Joel Myerson (Charlottesville: University Press of Virginia, 1991), 163–166.

32 Poe to William D. Ticknor, 23 December 1846, *Letters*, II: 335.

33 Poe to Philip P. Cooke, 9 August 1846, *Letters*, II: 329–330.

34 Poe to George W. Eveleth, 15 December 1846, *Letters*, II: 332–333.

35 Poe to George W. Eveleth, 15 December 1846, *Letters*, II: 333.

Bibliography

Alderman, Edwin A. "Edgar Allan Poe and the University of Virginia." *Virginia Quarterly Review* 1 (1925): 78–84.

Allen, Hervey. *Israfel: The Life and Times of Edgar Allan Poe*. New York: Farrar and Rinehart, 1934.

Allen, Michael. *Poe and the British Magazine Tradition*. New York: Oxford University Press, 1969.

Bandy, W. T. "Poe, Duane, and Duffee." *University of Mississippi Studies in English*, new ser. 3 (1982): 81–95.

Baudelaire, Charles. *Baudelaire on Poe*. Trans. and ed. Lois Hylsop and Francis E. Hylsop, Jr. State College, PA: Bald Eagle Press, 1952.

[Bennett, James Gordon.] "The Committee of the Booksellers." [New York] *Herald*, 13 April 1837.

"Great Literary Festival." [New York] *Herald*, 4 April 1837.

"Literary Taste." [New York] *Herald*, 4 May 1837.

Benton, Richard P. "The Tales: 1831–1835." In *A Companion to Poe Studies*. Ed. Eric W. Carlson. Westport, CT: Greenwood Press, 1996. 110–128.

Blanck, Jacob, and Michael Winship. *Bibliography of American Literature*. 9 vols. New Haven: Yale University Press, 1955–1991.

Bondurant, Agnes M. *Poe's Richmond*. Richmond: Garrett and Massie, 1942.

"Booksellers." *New-Yorker* 3 (1 April 1837): 29.

"Bookseller's Dinner." *Morning Courier and New-York Enquirer*, 1 April 1837.

"Booksellers' Festival." *New-York Daily Express*, 4 April 1837.

"Bookseller's Festival." [New York] *Evening Post*, 3 April 1837.

Bruce, Philip Alexander. "Background of Poe's University Life." *South Atlantic Quarterly* 10 (1911): 212–226.

History of the University of Virginia, 1819–1919. 5 vols. New York: Macmillan, 1920–1922.

Cameron, Kenneth Walter. "Notes on Young Poe's Reading." *American Transcendental Quarterly* no. 24 (Fall 1974): 33–34.

Campbell, Killis. "Poe's Reading: Addenda and Corrigenda." *University of Texas Studies in English* 7 (1927): 175–180.

Carlson, Eric W. *A Companion to Poe Studies*. Westport, CT: Greenwood Press, 1996.

Cauthen, I. B., Jr. "Poe's *Alone*: Its Background, Source, and Manuscript." *Studies in Bibliography* 3 (1950–1951): 284–291.

Chase, Lewis. "John Bransby, Poe's Schoolmaster." *Athenaeum*, no. 4605 (May 1916): 221–222.

Clemons, Harry. *The University of Virginia Library, 1825–1950: Story of a Jeffersonian Foundation*. Charlottesville: University of Virginia Library, 1954.

Colum, Padraic. Introduction. *Edgar Allan Poe's Tales of Mystery and Imagination*. London: J. M. Dent, 1916. vii–xv.

Davis, Richard Beale. *Intellectual Life in Jefferson's Virginia 1790–1830*. 1964. Reprinted. Knoxville: University of Tennessee Press, 1972.

Dickens, Charles. *The Letters of Charles Dickens: The Pilgrim Edition*. Ed. Kathleen Tillotson *et al.* 9 vols. to date. Oxford: Clarendon Press, 1965.

Dictionary of National Biography. Ed. Leslie Stephenson and Sidney Lee. 22 vols. Oxford: Oxford University Press, 1885–1901.

Dundes, Alan. "Some Examples of Infrequently Reported Autograph Verse." *Southern Folklore Quarterly* 26 (June 1962): 127–130.

Dunlop, G. B. "A Poe Story." *TLS* 15 January 1944, 36.

Duyckinck, Evert A. *Cyclopaedia of American Literature Embracing Personal and Critical Notices of Authors, and Selections from Their Writings*. 2 vols. New York: C. Scribner, 1855.

"Editor's Table." *Arthur's Ladies Magazine* 2 (November 1844): 242.

Elwell, T. E. "A Poe Story." *TLS* 23 October 1943, 516.

Exman, Eugene. *The Brothers Harper: A Unique Publishing Partnership and Its Impact upon the Cultural Life of America from 1817 to 1853*. New York: Harper and Row, 1965.

Fisher, Benjamin Franklin, IV. *The Very Spirit of Cordiality: The Literary Uses of Alcohol and Alcoholism in the Tales of Edgar Allan Poe*. Baltimore: Enoch Pratt Free Library and the Edgar Allan Poe Society, 1978.

Francis, John W. *Old New York: Or, Reminiscences of the Past Sixty Years*. New York: W. J. Widdleton, 1866.

Franklin, Benjamin. *Benjamin Franklin's Autobiography: A Norton Critical Edition*. Ed. J. A. Leo Lemay and P. M. Zall. New York: Norton, 1986.

French, John C. "Poe's Literary Baltimore." *Maryland Historical Magazine* 32 (1937): 101–112.

"Gil Blas and Don Quixote." *Athenaeum* (Boston) 8 (1 November 1820): 123.

Hatvary, George Egon. "Poe and the World of Books." In *A Companion to Poe Studies*. Ed. Eric W. Carlson. Westport, CT: Greenwood Press, 1996. 539–560.

Hawthorne, Nathaniel. *The American Notebooks*. Ed. Claude M. Simpson. Columbus: Ohio State University Press, 1971.

Hayes, Kevin J. *A Colonial Woman's Bookshelf*. Knoxville: University of Tennessee Press, 1996.

Folklore and Book Culture. Knoxville: University of Tennessee Press, 1997.

"Poe's Earliest Reading." *English Language Notes* 32 (March 1995): 39–43.

"Railway Reading." *Proceedings of the American Antiquarian Society* 106 (1997): 301–326.

"Thomas Powell Reviews Poe's *Literati*." *Poe Studies Association Newsletter* 22 (Spring 1995): 5.

Helm, Randel. "Another Source for Poe's *Arthur Gordon Pym*." *American Literature* 41 (January 1970): 572–575.

Hewitt, John Hill. *Shadows on the Wall: Or, Glimpses of the Past*. 1877. Reprinted. New York: AMS Press, 1971.

Hone, Philip. *The Diary of Philip Hone*. 2 vols. Ed. Bayard Tuckerman. New York: Dodd, Mead, 1889.

Hudson, Ruth Leigh. "Poe and Disraeli." *American Literature* 8 (January 1937): 402–416.

"Hume and Robertson Compared." *Port Folio*, ser. 3, vol. 4 (October 1810): 330.

Hunter, William Elijah. "Poe and His English Schoolmaster." *Athenaeum*, no. 2660 (19 October 1878): 496–497.

Jackson, David K. "Four of Poe's Critiques in the Baltimore Newspapers." *Modern Language Notes* 50 (April 1935): 251–256.

"A Man Named Bool: A Shadow on the Wall." *Poe Studies* 10 (December 1977): 44.

Jacobs, Robert D. *Poe: Journalist and Critic*. Baton Rouge: Louisiana State University Press, 1969.

Kaser, David. *A Book for a Sixpence: The Circulating Library in America*. Pittsburgh: Beta Phi Mu, 1980.

Keep, Austin Baxter. *History of the New York Society Library*. 1908. Reprinted. Boston: Gregg, 1972.

Kennedy, J. Gerald. *The Narrative of Arthur Gordon Pym and the Abyss of Interpretation*. New York: Twayne, 1995.

Kopley, Richard, ed. *Poe's Pym: Critical Explorations*. Durham: Duke University Press, 1992.

Lehmann-Haupt, Hellmut, Lawrence C. Wroth, and Rollo G. Silver. *The Book in America: A History of the Making and Selling of Books in the United States*. 2nd edn. New York: R. R. Bowker, 1952.

Lemay, J. A. Leo. "Poe's 'The Business Man': Its Contexts and Satire of Franklin's *Autobiography*." *Poe Studies* 15 (December 1982): 29–37.

Library Company of Baltimore. *A Catalogue of the Books*. Baltimore: Prentiss and Cole, 1802.

"A List of Books from Poe's Library." *Notes and Queries* 200 (1955): 222–223.

A Supplement to the Catalogue of Books. Baltimore: J. Robinson, 1816.

Ljungquist, Kent P. "Poe in the Boston Newspapers: Three More Reviews." *English Language Notes* 31.2 (1993):43–45.

Lyell, Charles. *A Second Visit to the United States of North America*. 2 vols. New York: Harper and Brothers, 1849.

Mabbott, Thomas Ollive "Evidence that Poe Knew Greek." *Notes and Queries* 185 (17 July 1943): 39–40.

McLuhan, Herbert Marshall. "Edgar Poe's Tradition." *Sewanee Review* 52 (January 1944): 24–33.

Melville, Herman. *Pierre: Or, The Ambiguities.* Ed. Harrison Hayford, Hershel Parker, and G. Thomas Tanselle. Evanston and Chicago: Northwestern University Press and The Newberry Library, 1971.

Moore, Thomas. *The Poetical Works of Thomas Moore.* Ed. A. D. Godley. New York: Oxford University Press, 1924.

Mott, Frank Luther. *Golden Multitudes: The Story of Best Sellers in the United States.* New York: Macmillan, 1947.

A History of American Magazines 1741–1850. 5 vols. Cambridge: The Belknap Press of Harvard University Press, 1930–1968.

"Narrative of Arthur Gordon Pym, of Nantucket, North America." *Court Gazette and Fashionable Guide* 1 (13 October 1838): 445.

National Union Catalog: Pre-1956 Imprints. 754 vols. London: Mansell, 1968–1981.

Neal, John. *Randolph, A Novel.* 2 vols. N.p.: n.p., 1823.

Wandering Recollections of a Somewhat Busy Life: An Autobiography. Boston: Roberts Brothers, 1869.

"New-York Booksellers' Dinner." *American Monthly Magazine,* new ser. 3 (May 1837): 521–524.

Nichols, Mary Gove. *Reminiscences of Edgar Allan Poe.* 1929. Reprinted. New York: Haskall House, 1974.

Norman, Emma Katherine. "Poe's Knowledge of Latin." *American Literature* 6 (March 1934): 72–77.

"Novels of the Month." *Monthly Review* 3 (October 1838): 560–569.

Parks, Edd Winfield. *Edgar Allan Poe as Literary Critic.* Athens: University of Georgia Press, 1964.

Peacock, Thomas Love. *The Poems of Thomas Love Peacock.* Ed. Brimley Johnson. London: George Routledge and Sons, n.d.

Poe, Edgar Allan. "Armstrong's Notices." *Southern Literary Messenger* 2 (June 1836): 450–451.

The Brevities: Pinakidia, Marginalia, Fifty Suggestions, and Other Works. Ed. Burton R. Pollin. New York: Gordian Press, 1985.

Collected Works of Edgar Allan Poe. Ed. Thomas Ollive Mabbott. 3 vols. Cambridge: Belknap Press of Harvard University Press, 1969–1978.

Complete Works of Edgar Allan Poe. Ed. James A. Harrison. 17 vols. 1902. Reprinted. New York: AMS, 1965.

"Critical Notices and Literary Intelligence." *Southern Literary Messenger* 1 (August 1835): 714–716.

Edgar Allan Poe: Essays and Reviews. Ed. G. R. Thompson. New York: Library of America, 1984.

Edgar Allan Poe: Poetry and Tales. Ed. Patrick F. Quinn. New York: Library of America, 1984.

"Emilia Harrington." *Southern Literary Messenger* 2 (February 1836): 191–192.

"Erato." *Southern Literary Messenger* 2 (July 1836): 513–514.

["Exordium."] *Graham's Magazine* 20 (January 1842): 68.

"Godwin's Necromancy." *Southern Literary Messenger* 2 (December 1835): 65.

The Imaginary Voyages: The Narrative of Arthur Gordon Pym, The Unparalleled Adventure of One Hans Pfaall, The Journal of Julius Rodman. Ed. Burton R. Pollin. Boston: Twayne, 1981.

The Letters of Edgar Allan Poe. Ed. John Ward Ostrom. 1948. Reprinted, with supplement. 2 vols. New York: Gordian Press, 1966.

"Nuts to Crack." *Southern Literary Messenger* 2 (December 1835): 49.

"Paul Ulric." *Southern Literary Messenger* 2 (February 1836): 173–180.

Politan: An Unfinished Tragedy. Ed. Thomas Ollive Mabbott. Menasha, WI: Collegiate Press, 1923.

"Professor Dew's Address." *Southern Literary Messenger* 2 (October 1836): 721–722.

"Recollections of Coleridge." *Southern Literary Messenger* 2 (June 1836): 451–453.

Review of John Quincy Adams, *The Jubilee of the Constitution. Burton's Gentleman's Magazine* 5 (August 1839): 114.

Review of Charles Anthon, ed., *Select Orations of Cicero: with an English Commentary and Historical, Geographical and Legal Indexes. Southern Literary Messenger* 3 (January 1837): 72.

Review of Delia S. Bacon, *The Bride of Fort Edward. Burton's Gentleman's Magazine* 5 (September 1839): 168–169.

Review of William Beckford, *Recollections of an Excursion to the Monasteries of Alcobaca and Batalha. Southern Literary Messenger* 1 (August 1835): 714.

Review of Robert M. Bird, *Hawks of Hawk-Hollow; A Tradition of Pennsylvania, Southern Literary Messenger* 2 (December 1835): 43–46.

Review of Benvenuto Cellini, *Memoirs of Benvenuto Cellini. Broadway Journal* 2 (1 November 1845): 257.

Review of Lydia Maria Child, *Philothea: A Romance. Broadway Journal* 1 (24 May 1845): 342–345.

Review of Lydia Maria Child, *Philothea: A Romance. Southern Literary Messenger* 2 (September 1836): 659–662.

Review of *The Gift. Southern Literary Messenger* 1 (September 1835): 780.

Review of Charles Fenno Hoffman, *A Winter in the West. Southern Literary Messenger* 1 (April 1835): 459.

Review of Washington Irving, *A Tour on the Prairies. Southern Literary Messenger* 1 (April 1835): 456–457.

Review of John Pendleton Kennedy, *Horse Shoe Robinson: A Tale of the Tory Ascendancy. Southern Literary Messenger* 1 (May 1835): 522–524.

Review of *London Quarterly Review. Southern Literary Messenger* 1 (April 1835): 458.

Review of Alessandro Manzoni, *I Promessi Sposi*, trans. G. W. Featherstonhaugh. *Southern Literary Messenger* 1 (May 1835): 520–522.

Review of Frederick Marryat, *The Phantom Ship*. *Burton's Gentleman's Magazine* 5 (August 1839): 358–359.

Review of *North American Review* (51 [October 1835]). *Southern Literary Messenger* 2 (December 1835): 63–64.

Review of James Pedder, *Frank*. *Burton's Gentleman's Magazine* 6 (May 1840): 250.

Review of Hugh A. Pue, *Grammar of the English Language*. *Graham's Magazine* 19 (July 1841): 45.

Review of *Sallust's Jugurthine War*, ed. Charles Anthon. *Southern Literary Messenger* 2 (May 1836): 392–393.

Review of B. B. Thatcher, *Traits of the Tea Party*. *Southern Literary Messenger* 2 (March 1836): 292.

Review of Frances Trollope, *Paris and the Parisians in 1835*. *Southern Literary Messenger* 2 (May 1836): 393–396.

Review of Robert Folkestone Williams, *Mephistopheles in England, Or The Confessions of a Prime Minister*. *Southern Literary Messenger* 1 (September 1835): 776–777.

"The Southern Literary Messenger." *Broadway Journal* 1 (22 March 1845): 183.

Tamerlane and Other Poems. Boston: Calvin F. S. Thomas, 1827.

Writings in The Broadway Journal: Nonfictional Prose. Ed. Burton R. Pollin. 2 vols. New York: Gordian, 1986.

Pollin, Burton R. "The Living Writers of America: A Manuscript by Edgar Allan Poe." In *Studies in the American Renaissance, 1991*. Ed. Joel Myerson. Charlottesville: University Press of Virginia, 1991. 151–212.

"Poe and Daniel Defoe: A Significant Relationship." *Topic* 30 (Fall 1976): 3–22.

"Poe's Life Reflected through the Sources of *Pym*." In *Poe's Pym: Critical Explorations*. Ed. Richard Kopley. Durham: Duke University Press, 1992. 95–103.

Potter, Charles Francis. "Round Went the Album." *New York Folklore Quarterly* 4 (Spring 1948): 5–14.

"Public Dinner of the Booksellers and Publishers." *Albion* 5 (1 April 1837): 103.

Quinn, Arthur Hobson. *Edgar Allan Poe: A Critical Biography*. 1941. Reprinted. Baltimore: Johns Hopkins University Press, 1998.

Randolph, Vance, and May Kennedy McCord. "Autograph Albums in the Ozarks." *Journal of American Folklore* 61 (1948): 182–193.

Reiman, Donald H. *The Study of Modern Manuscripts: Public, Confidential, and Private*. Baltimore: Johns Hopkins University Press, 1993.

Review of *The Narrative of Arthur Gordon Pym*. [New York] *Albion*, new ser. 6 (18 August 1838): 263.

Review of *The Narrative of Arthur Gordon Pym*. *Metropolitan Magazine* 23 (November 1838): 81.

Review of *The Raven and Other Poems*. *Anglo-American* 6 (22 November 1845): 116.

Rhizoid, Christina. *The Letters of Christina Rhizoid*. Vol. 1. Ed. Anthony H. Harrison. Charlottesville: University Press of Virginia, 1997.

Rogers, Joseph W. "The Rise of American Edition Binding." In *Bookbinding in America*. Ed. Hellmut Lehmann-Haupt. New York: Bowker, 1967. 131–185.

Sadleir, Michael. *XIX Century Fiction: A Bibliographical Record*. 2 vols. Berkeley: University of California Press, 1951.

Scharf, J. Thomas. *History of Baltimore City and County*. 1881. Reprinted. Baltimore: Regional Publishing Company, 1971.

Schick, Frank L. *The Paperbound Book in America: The History of Paperbacks and Their European Background*. New York: R. R. Bowker, 1958.

Schultz, Heidi M. "Edgar Allan Poe Submits 'The Bells' to *Sartain's Magazine*." *Resources for American Literary Study* 22 (1996): 166–181.

Scott, Walter. "Life and Character of Le Sage." *Museum of Foreign Literature and Science* 5 (October 1824): 297–316.

Sealts, Merton M., Jr. *Melville's Reading: Revised and Enlarged Edition*. Columbia: University of South Carolina Press, 1988.

Semmes, John E. *John H. B. Latrobe and His Times, 1803–1891*. Baltimore: Norman, Remington, 1917.

Shaw, George Bernard. "Edgar Allan Poe." *Nation* 4 (16 January 1909):601–602.

Sherman, Stuart C. "The Library Company of Baltimore, 1795–1854." *Maryland Historical Magazine* 39 (March 1944): 6–24.

Shove, Raymond Howard. *Cheap Book Production in the United States, 1870–1891*. Urbana: University of Illinois Library, 1937.

Silver, Rollo G. "The Baltimore Book Trade, 1800–1825." *Bulletin of the New York Public Library* 57 (1953): 114–125, 182–201, 248–251, 297–305, 349–357.

Sowerby, E. Millicent. *Catalogue of the Library of Thomas Jefferson*. 1952–1959. Reprinted. 5 vols. Charlottesville: University Press of Virginia, 1983.

Stanard, Mary Newton, ed. *Edgar Allan Poe Letters Till Now Unpublished in the Valentine Museum, Richmond, Virginia*. 1925. Reprinted. New York: Haskell House, 1973.

Stoddard, Roger E. *"Put a Resolute Hart to a Steep Hill": William Gowans, Antiquary and Bookseller*. New York: Book Arts Press of the School of Library Service, Columbia University, 1990.

Stokes, Isaac Newton Phelps. *The Iconography of Manhattan Island, 1498–1909*. 6 vols. New York: Robert H. Dodd, 1915–1928.

Stovall, Floyd. "Edgar Poe and the University of Virginia." *Virginia Quarterly Review* 43 (Spring 1967): 297–317.

"Supplement to the Southern Literary Messenger." *Southern Literary Messenger* 2 (January 1836): 133–140.

Tebbel, John. *A History of Book Publishing in the United States.* 4 vols. New York: R. R. Bowker, 1972–1981.

Thomas, Dwight, and David K. Jackson. *The Poe Log: A Documentary Life of Edgar Allan Poe 1809–1849.* Boston: G. K. Hall, 1987.

Thompson, G. R. *Poe's Fiction: Romantic Irony in the Gothic Tales.* Madison: University of Wisconsin Press, 1973.

Uhler, John Earle. "The Delphian Club: A Contribution to the Literary History of Baltimore in the Early Nineteenth Century." *Maryland Historical Magazine* 20 (December 1925): 305–346.

Vanderbilt, Kermit. *American Literature and the Academy: The Roots, Growth, and Maturity of a Profession.* Philadelphia: University of Pennsylvania Press, 1986.

"Variety." *Port Folio* new ser. 1 (25 January 1806): 44–45.

Ward, A. W., and A. R. Waller. *The Cambridge History of English Literature.* Vol. xiv. New York: G. P. Putnam's Sons, 1917.

Weiner, Bruce I. *The Most Noble of Professions: Poe and the Poverty of Authorship.* Baltimore: The Enoch Pratt Free Library, the Edgar Allan Poe Society and the Library of the University of Baltimore, 1987.

"Novels, Tales, and Problems of Form in *The Narrative of Arthur Gordon Pym*." In Kepley, *Poe's Pym,* 44–56.

Wilmer, Lambert A. *Our Press Gang; or, A Complete Exposition of the Corruptions and Crimes of the American Newspapers.* Philadelphia: J. T. Lloyd, 1859.

The Quacks of Helicon. Philadelphia: J. W. Macclefield, 1841.

"Recollections of Edgar A. Poe." In Lambert A. Wilmer, *Merlin: Baltimore, 1827.* Ed. Thomas Ollive Mabbott. New York: Scholars' Facsimiles and Reprints, 1941. 29–34.

Wilson, James Grant. *The Memorial History of the City of New-York from Its First Settlement to the Year 1892.* 5 vols. New York: New-York History Company, 1893.

Wilson, James Southall. "The Devil Was in It." *American Mercury* 24 (October 1931):215–220.

Wolf, Edwin, ii. "Horace Wemyss Smith's Recollections of Poe." *Library Chronicle of the University of Pennsylvania* 17 (Summer 1951):90–103.

Wroth, Lawrence C. "Poe's Baltimore." *Johns Hopkins Alumni Magazine* 17 (June 1929):299–312.

X.L.O., "The Mission of Novelettes." *Holden's Dollar Monthly* 1 (April 1848): 218.

Index